Papermaking on the Water of Leith

Flashbacks

Other SAPPHIRE titles in the Flashbacks series include

Thomas Nelson and Sons: Memories of an Edinburgh Publishing House
Edited by Heather Holmes and David Finkelstein

Papermaking on the Water of Leith

Edited by

Alistair McCleery,
David Finkelstein and Sarah Bromage

JOHN DONALD

in association with
SAPPHIRE: Scottish Archive of Print and
Publishing History Records

First published in Great Britain in 2006 by
John Donald, an imprint of Birlinn Ltd

West Newington House
10 Newington Road
Edinburgh
EH9 1QS

www.birlinn.co.uk

ISBN 10: 0 85976 672 1
ISBN 13: 978 0 85976 672 2

Copyright © SAPPHIRE, Napier University 2006

All rights reserved. No part of this publication may
be reproduced, stored or transmitted in any form, or
by any means, electronic, mechanical or photocopying,
recording or otherwise, without the express written
permission of the publisher.

British Library Cataloguing-in-Publication Data
A catalogue record for this book is
available from the British Library

Typeset by Hewer Text UK Ltd, Edinburgh
Printed and bound in Britain by Bell and Bain Ltd, Glasgow

Contents

Map of the Water of Leith	vi
Mill Sites	vii
Preface	xi
Acknowledgements	xiv
Introduction Alistair McCleery	xvi
Biographies	xxv
Jim White	1
Kate Milne	42
Nan Aitken	60
'Mary Reid'	69
Thallon Veitch	83
Richard Blaikie	112
William Nelson	135
Glossary	162

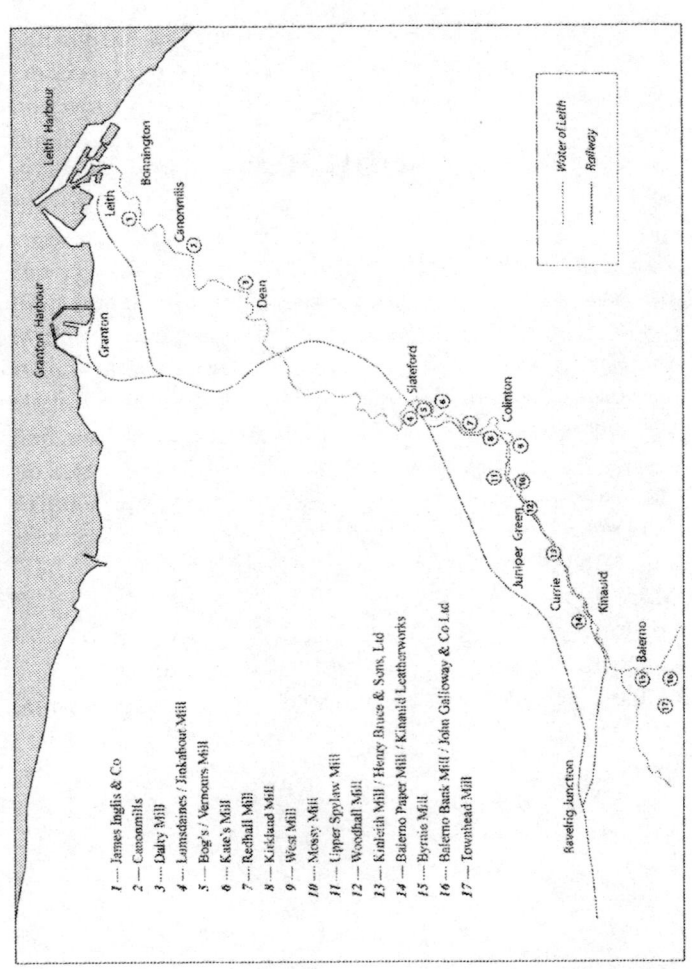

Mill Sites

1. James Inglis & Co
   This mill specialising in boards, wrappers and crayon papers began operation in 1889. The Williamson family owned it until 1987 when Stirling Fibre took it over. When it closed in 1989, Inglis Mill was the last papermill in operation on the Water of Leith.

2. Canonmills
   The first record of this mill is 1659 when it is recorded that the mill was visited by Edinburgh dignitaries. In 1681 Peter Bruce of Canonmills was given a monopoly for the manufacture of playing cards, and in 1682 he was appointed the King's printer. Shortly after this elevation he gave up the mill.

3. Dalry Mill
   The first papermill in Scotland was started in 1590 at Dalry, and in 1594 it was given an eleven-year lease to produce paper. There are no further records of the mill until 1675 when Alex Daes took over the production of paper on the site. The mill is now part of Roseburn House.

4. Lumsdaines / Jinkabout Mill
   This site was first used as a mill in 1506. Between 1714 and 1737 the mill produced paper, but it was converted

to grind and prepare barley between 1737 and 1755. Jinkabout Mill was then demolished for the construction of a kitchen garden.

5. Bog's / Vernours Mill
   A waulk mill was situated here from 1598, but by 1717 paper was being produced at the mill. In 1816 Bog's Mill was converted to a snuff, grain and spice mill. It continued production until 1924 when the mill burned to the ground. There is now a private house on the site of this mill.

6. Waulk Mill of Colinton / Kate's Mill
   This mill began production as a waulk mill in 1518. In 1783 John Balfour was granted a fifty-seven-year lease for the production of paper. Balfour named the mill after his wife, Catherine Cant of Thurston, and the mill continued production until 1890.

7. Redhall Mill
   In 1718 Redhall began making paper for banknotes. The mill had a large kitchen on the ground floor that catered for the bank directors who holidayed in Colinton while the notes were being made. In 1742 the mill changed to the processing of barley and later became a plastics factory. In 1970 Redhall Mill was converted into flats.

8. Kirkland Mill
   This mansion house was converted into a lint mill in 1777. It subsequently changed use many times, including being employed as a meal and snuff mill. In 1870 Kirkland Mill was converted to a board mill.

MILL SITES

9. West Mill
From 1699 this mill undertook three production activities: waulking, the processing of grain and the production of linen. In 1799 the mill began production of paper. However, from 1909 to 1971 the mill solely produced grain.

10. Mossy Mill / Wester Waulk Mill
In 1595 Wester Waulk Mill was leased by Imbre and Alex Mosie. By 1664 it had been renamed Mossy Mill, after William Mosie or Mosey. Cloth was beetled at Mossie Mill until 1838 when it was converted to a papermill by Mr McWhirter, who was also a tenant of Inglis Green. The mill made wrappings until it closed in 1972.

11. Upper Spylaw Mill
This mill produced paper between 1682 and 1765. In 1765 it became a snuff mill; by 1880 the site was used as a dairy and latterly as a riding stable.

12. Woodhall Mill
Woodhall began its industrial life as a waulk mill in 1677. It was briefly used as a lint mill between 1779 and 1792 when it became a papermill producing wrappings and browns. Woodhall was taken over by Inveresk in 1954 and in 1957 was converted into a board mill producing board for the whisky industry, among others. Woodhall ceased production in 1984.

13. Kinleith Mill / Henry Bruce & Sons, Ltd
A mill had been located on this site from 1618, but there is no record of its use until 1792 when it began producing paper. In 1844 Kinleith was bought by Henry Bruce. In 1928 the mill was absorbed into the Inveresk

company and was producing featherweight book papers. However, in 1966 Inveresk closed Kinleith and moved the production of bookpapers elsewhere.

14. Balerno Paper Mill / Kinauld Leatherworks
In 1770 Nisbet and MacNiven founded Balerno Mill. By 1793 the *Statistical Account* refers to the mill as 'perhaps the most extensive on one waterfall of any at present in the island' making brown and cartridge paper. In 1875 Balerno Mill burned down and the buildings were used as storage space until 1904 when it became a glue works. From 1913 until the beginning of the present century it was the site of a working tannery.

15. Byrnie Mill
Byrnie Mill produced tea and grey paper between 1799 and 1905. In 1905 it was converted to a sawmill.

16. Balerno Bank Mill / John Galloway & Sons
Balerno Bank Mill began producing tea paper, grey paper and printings in 1805. In 1909 the mill burned down, but it was rebuilt and reopened in 1912. In 1925 it was bought by John Galloway, who began the production of high-quality art paper. The firm ceased production in 1971.

17. Townhead Mill
In 1825 William Blaikie was registered as the owner and tenant of this one-vat papermill making tea and grey paper. In 1832 James Bain was registered as the owner of the mill and this site was incorporated into Balerno Bank. By 1842, the mill was being used as a storehouse for rags. It later became a private house.

Preface

THE Papermaking on the Water of Leith project was an initiative of the Scottish Archive of Print and Publishing History Records (SAPPHIRE). SAPPHIRE aims to capture the social, economic and cultural history of the Scottish printing and publishing industry in the twentieth century and to document aspects of the working lives of people who have been employed within the industry and witnessed the changes that have taken place there. SAPPHIRE is a collaborative venture between Napier University and Queen Margaret University College, both based in Edinburgh; SAPPHIRE also works in collaboration with a number of other universities in the UK and overseas, with organisations active in oral history, with the printing and publishing industry, and with heritage institutions. The recordings, photographs, films and ephemera gathered from a number of projects form the SAPPHIRE archive held at Napier University; this archive has provided, in turn, the material for exhibitions, publications and learning resource packs for schools. Further details can be found on our website, www.sapphire.ac.uk.

This book includes representative examples of interviews undertaken during the course of the Papermaking on the Water of Leith project. Although the papermaking industry was a significant component of the Scottish economy and had had a major impact in shaping the communities where it was based, little was known about its history in the twentieth century. There are few company records that document this period and no material that charts the working lives of the men and women who worked in the mills. SAPPHIRE initiated the Papermaking on the Water of Leith project specifically to fill these gaps in knowledge and understanding through recording the testimonies of the employees of the papermills on this river. The project began in June 2002 when a reunion of former papermill employees was held at the Water of Leith Visitor Centre in Edinburgh. Over thirty individuals who had worked in the mills along the river attended this reminiscence session. Individual interviews followed, and new contacts were made who also shared their memories of life within the papermaking industry. Photographs and home movies were collected, as were examples of some of the ephemera of working life, such as a letter of appointment or a menu from a 'flannel dance'.

Papermills on the Water of Leith were largely family-owned concerns. Many of these had been producing paper for centuries. They were the largest employers of labour in their respective areas and drew their workforces from the villages surrounding the mills, often employing several generations from the same family. The role these mills played in their respective communities cannot be over-estimated. As one interviewee noted, anyone walking through Currie and Juniper Green during the years when the mills were at their peak would get a sense that 'if the mill chimney was smoking, everything was good. If the mill chimney wasn't smoking, then something was wrong.' The mills dominated the skyline with their tall lums. The owners provided housing for their employees, built and ran re-

PREFACE

creational facilities, and sponsored annual trips and dances.

This book draws on the reminiscences of seven individuals who worked in three of the largest mills on the Water of Leith: the mill of John Galloway & Sons in Balerno, the Kinleith Mill of Henry Bruce & Sons in Currie, and Woodhall Mill in Juniper Green. These represent a range of mills and the interviewees cover a diversity of work roles – from laboratory technicians and office employees to the salle workers and machine men who made the actual paper. The interviews document work in the mills, technological change and innovations in the papermaking industry, the range of paper and paper products produced along the Water of Leith, the impact of mill activity on the river communities, and the effect of the demise of the papermills.

When Inglis Mill closed in 1989, it signalled the end of an industry that had been active on the Water of Leith for nearly 400 years. As one interviewee concludes, there was a great sense of loss felt in the surrounding villages when the mills slowly began to disappear during the 1970s and 1980s. 'I think one of the saddest things was seeing these great lorries taking away the machinery. I can remember standing at the [school] staffroom window and watching the papermaking machines going down the village. You felt that the heart had gone out the village, and the village has never been the same.'

Acknowledgements

WE wish to record our immense debt of gratitude to all the former employees of the papermills who kindly shared their memories of life and work in the mills on the Water of Leith and provided invaluable advice and guidance that helped to shape the project. In particular, we would like to single out William Nelson, Kate Milne, 'Mary Reid', Nan Aitken, Jim White, Richard Blaikie and Thallon Veitch, who all set aside considerable time to assist with the compilation of this volume.

We would also like to recognise the necessary inspiration of Dr Heather Holmes in suggesting the Water of Leith as a topic for research and to thank her and the other members of the SAPPHIRE advisory panel for their counsel and encouragement during the development and implementation of the project. The members of staff of the Water of Leith Visitor Centre were ever co-operative and concerned for the success of the project. In addition, we are grateful to the members of staff at the Archive, Records Management and Museum Service at Heriot-Watt University for access to the Tweedie Collection and for permission to use its photographic archive. Bette More also kindly allowed us to use her photographs. Ian Gunn was helpful and supportive over and beyond the call of friendship in preparing maps and other exhibition materials.

ACKNOWLEDGEMENTS

This project has only been made possible by the generous support of the Heritage Lottery Fund's 'Your Heritage' scheme, The Pilgrim Trust, The Russell Trust, and John Lewis plc. We wish to express our thanks to all these organisations without whose assistance the Papermaking on the Water of Leith project would not have been completed so successfully. Finally, we would like to acknowledge the assistance of The Russell Trust, Stirling Fibre Ltd, Napier University and the QMUC Innovations Fund in the publication of this volume.

Introduction

> Thou hast most traitorously corrupted the youth of the realm in erecting a grammar school; and, whereas, before, our forefathers had no other books but the score and the tally, thou hast caused printing to be used; and contrary to the King, his crown and dignity, thou hast built a paper-mill.
>
> *Henry VI*

THE founders of the first papermill in Scotland, at Dalry on the Water of Leith in 1590, may not have been wholly aware of their participation in the three-legged revolution of education, printing and papermaking, but they would have been conscious of a new spirit abroad in a post-Reformation nation that placed great emphasis upon literacy and the availability of the Word of God. The establishment of the mill would have been a commercial response to the demand for the paper that the development of an educated civil and religious society required. The location provided the clean, flowing water needed for both the motive power of the mill and the papermaking process itself. Proximity to the relatively large conurbation of Edinburgh facilitated the collection of linen rags that constituted the primary raw material in that process. The Water of Leith stretches for some 24 miles from the Pent-

INTRODUCTION

land Hills, located to the south of the city, and the villages of Currie, Balerno and Colinton to the port of Leith to the north and the river's emergence into the Firth of Forth (see map of the Water of Leith, p. vi). By the mid-nineteenth century, some eighty mills drew on it for power and water; many of these were papermills, creating a Cellulose Glen that supplied the basic material for Scotland's cultural and scientific successes for almost 400 years. The mills also created tightly knit communities, guided by the paternalism of the mill owners, in which generations of the same family would work in the mill, live in tied housing and spend their time off in facilities provided by their employers. Edinburgh could seem an impossible distance away in miles and in outlook.

Even further away lay the origins of the industry. Papermaking was invented in China at the beginning of the second century AD (examples survive from between 150 and 200) and slowly spread westwards through Kashmir and Persia, reaching the Arab states of North Africa by the eleventh century. From there the Arabs introduced it to Spain where a papermill was operating in Toledo in 1085. The craft had reached France by 1190 and Italy by 1276. The Nile had throughout antiquity provided a different kind of writing material – papyrus. From at least 3500 BC, rolls were being made from this marsh grass found in the river delta. Pliny's account of their manufacture describes two strips of flattened papyrus stem being overlaid at right-angles and pressed together on a damp board. The natural gum of the plant released by the pressing bonded the layers and, once dried, up to twenty of these compact sheets (each about 16 inches long) could be pasted together to form a roll. A finished papyrus roll was fine-grained, firm, white and smooth, ready to be daubed with black and red inks using a frayed reed brush. Papyrus served the Ptolemaic rulers of Egypt but also became the dominant writing material of the Greek and Roman empires.

However, papyrus grew only on the Nile and, as the use of writing spread, the limits of the plant's supply led to the production of parchment. Animal skins had long been used as a writing surface but, like wood or bark, they were perishable. A papyrus shortage in Asia Minor in the second century BC stimulated skin preparation to the point where a durable material able to be written on both sides and less fragile than papyrus was developed. The lime-soaked skins of sheep, goats and calves (vellum) were scraped of their hair and flesh and stretched on a frame to be chalked and dried. The advantages over papyrus meant that by the fourth century AD parchment had become the predominant writing material in Europe and continued to be so until the coming of paper from 1085 onwards. According to the paper historian Dard Hunter, paper is distinguished from other writing materials such as papyrus or parchment by a process of maceration: the soaking and breakdown of the raw material until the fibre of the original becomes individual filaments that can then be pressed into thin sheets. Cellulose is a polymer: that is, a substance with a long, strong molecular chain, which gives these thin sheets a seemingly disproportionate strength.

The initial papermaking process involved the collection of cellulose in the form of old rags (by rag-and-bone men) that were taken to the mill to be sorted, chopped and steeped in water. Grinding of the resultant mixture was followed by further soaking in a vat of soapy water until the fibres separated into the individual filaments and created a pulp. This was scooped into a brass-latticed, wooden-framed screen from which the water drained, leaving a

INTRODUCTION

layer or sheet of matted fibres that could be dried, pressed, sized and hung. During the first stage of pressing under a screw-press, sheets were placed on pieces of felt that absorbed the moisture. These are the 'felts' that play a significant role in the memories of some of the interviewees included in this selection. The sheets were then pressed against each other, which produced a smoother finish. Sizing involved coating the paper in a starchy liquid to make it less absorbent of ink. The fundamentals of this process remained unchanged until mechanisation of the industry in the early nineteenth century.

Nine hundred years previously, trade across the Mediterranean with Muslim Spain brought papermaking to northern Italy, principally through the port of Genoa. But it was the technological improvements made by Italians that turned Fabriano at the end of the thirteenth century into the papermaking centre of Europe. By introducing spiked mallets to tear and pound the rags instead of grindstones, by growing flax and hemp which gave a better rag base, and by using animal glue and gelatine for sizing rather than vegetable glues, the papermakers of Fabriano both improved the quality of the paper and increased output. During the fourteenth century the Fabriano business expanded, setting up mills at Voltri, Padua, Treviso and Genoa. Italian papermakers were such a force in the industry that they soon began establishing mills in France, Switzerland and Germany.

These mills tended to be located upriver, as on the Water of Leith, or at the fringes of mountain regions in order to access fast-running, relatively clear water to turn the mill and soak the pulp. For precisely these reasons the Vosges established itself as a papermaking region in France, and here the industry also benefited from the prevailing manufacture of linen, which helped in the supply of raw material. Mills needed to be close to trade routes – rivers were also, therefore, of importance in the distribution of the finished product – and near centres of consumption, such as administrative, legal and educational focal points like Edinburgh. The first English mill of which records exist was established at Hertford around 1490; as noted above, the first Scottish papermill does not appear until a century later. This hiatus, as with the first printer in Edinburgh in 1507, may be accounted for by a number of factors, not least the relative poverty of Scotland, its openness to imports and the lack of growth in a literate culture, outside court and church, until the Reformation.

The linen or cotton rags that were the most common raw material used in papermaking until the nineteenth century were generally cheap and fairly easy to come by – although a shortage in the seventeenth century led the English parliament to prohibit the burial of the dead in linen or cotton shrouds. Rags would be treated by washing and removing any hooks or buttons before the papermaking process could begin, something referred to in the interviews that follow. These rags would be partially dissolved in water to produce a fermented pulp (or 'stock'); they may have been pounded with mortars until they had reached the desired consistency. A size such as starch or glue might be added to the stock in order to make it smooth and less porous for printing or writing. The pulp would have been transferred to a mould by the 'vatman' using a dipping motion; the size of the paper sheet would be limited to the size of mould the vatman could carry. Papermaking moulds are trays made of closely woven wire surrounded by a deckle that stops the pulp slopping out of the mould. The mould would then be 'couched', pressed onto a

INTRODUCTION

woollen felt so that the mould could be used for the next piece of paper. The 'coucher' would stack the sheets, each divided by a woollen felt until there were sufficient to be put into a screw-press to remove most of the remaining water. The paper would then be pressed a second time and subsequently hung up to dry. Paper made by hand is now considered an art product and is used for limited purposes; it is still identifiable by its distinctive deckle edge and lack of grain, but its twin disadvantages are its cost and its lack of uniformity.

By the start of the nineteenth century, those working in the industry were beginning to experiment with mechanisation of the process to alleviate those disadvantages. The introduction of machinery into the papermills would revolutionise a process that was labour-intensive and prone to inaccuracy in a similar manner to changes brought about more generally in manufacturing by the Industrial Revolution. It would also promote social changes, in particular the creation of mill villages where work and community, life each day from cradle to grave, would focus on and be determined by the mill.

In 1798 Nicolas Louis Robert in Revolutionary France invented a moving wire-mesh belt that would receive a flow of pulp from the vat, shaking it from side to side and causing the cellulose filaments to bind, before transferring it to spinning rolls that would then squeeze out the water. The principles of this machine allowed paper to be made to any length and to a width limited only by the width of the wire mesh. Engineers in the employ of the Fourdrinier brothers, two London stationers of French origin, expanded upon Robert's ideas, and the Fourdrinier machine was patented in 1807. A variation of the Fourdrinier brothers' machine is still used in modern papermills, and its origins account for many of the French terms, such as 'salle', peppered throughout these interviews. The Fourdrinier machine consists initially of a headbox that emits a steady flow of pulp over the length and width of the proposed sheet, ensuring an evenly produced paper. The process is continued in the Fourdrinier table, where the pulp is laid evenly and where drainage begins to take place. The press section follows, where the paper is evenly squeezed between two felts and loses more water. The paper is moved on to the dryer section and is carried through rotating dryers. The size press then imparts some component such as glue or starch to improve the surface of the paper. The paper is smoothed still further on rotating heated cylinders, or 'calenders', and on to the reel. This is cut up into the appropriate length of sheets that are then traditionally counted into reams. The Fourdrinier brothers were able to increase their production of paper tenfold, from an output of 60–100 lb per day produced by hand to 1,000 lb per day using their new machine. Fifty years after the mechanisation of the process, at the beginning of the Victorian period, the price of paper had dropped by almost one half.

The nineteenth century saw further innovation in the papermaking process through the introduction of wood pulps and esparto grass, and the general phasing out of rags, as the raw material for paper. Esparto grass in particular became a key raw material for the mills on the Water of Leith, as these interviews reveal. Esparto was tough enough to survive the harsh climate of southern Spain and North Africa and provided a cheap and plentiful source of cellulose fibre. Bales of the grass were shipped into Granton docks for use in the papermaking process on the Water of Leith. The lorries sped up the hills of Edin-

INTRODUCTION

burgh, spreading loose strands of grass as they went, through the Bridges and Tollcross to Balerno and Currie. Henry Bruce's Kinleith Mill at Currie was one of the first mills on the Water of Leith to use esparto grass as a raw material. The company had been approached by the Edinburgh printers T. and A. Constable to produce a lightweight bulky paper for novels. By using esparto grass, the Kinleith Mill made a 24/32 bulk basis paper and featherweight paper was born.

The most common raw materials used in contemporary papermaking are wood, rags, waste paper and paperboard. However, to create specialist finishes new ingredients have been added to papers such as asphalt, synthetic adhesives, metal foils, plastic and cellulose films and coatings, and ink. These new additives can create problems for those involved in paper recovery systems. The recycling of paper has grown in popularity in the last few decades in the interests of the environment. Reused paper stock now counts for a large percentage of the total output of papers and almost all that of paperboards and box boards.

As the hand press was superseded by the rotary press, a need developed for paper to be supplied to the printer in rolls rather than in sheets. These 'webs' of paper are now most commonly used and are essential for techniques such as offset lithography. However, most of the main technical developments in papermaking had already occurred by the end of the nineteenth century. The subsequent century saw a process of refinement rather than innovation. The two world wars were the source of most concern for paper suppliers and purchasers in the twentieth century. The outbreak of war in 1914 and its attendant problems of import and export deepened the supply difficulties that had already been apparent in the first decade of the century. The Board of Trade rationed paper to all but essential publishing business. Answering the protestations of the Publishers' Association, paper was still provided for textbook manufacture. As paper became scare and its price shot up, there was an attendant rise in the prices of books. The Second World War saw the recurrence of many of the problems of the First. As Britain imported almost all raw materials for papermaking, the industry was hit badly. Paper was rationed in 1940, and the publishing of books decreased dramatically. However, paperbacks benefited from this reduced competition: their economical printing techniques meant that more books could be produced from a smaller amount of a lesser-grade paper.

The interviews recorded in this book reflect experiences shaped by the decades subsequent to the end of the Second World War. They show how the papermaking mills along the Water of Leith were embedded within the fabric of the local community. The individuals whose stories are shared in this volume talk forthrightly about their times in an industry going through significant changes in the second half of the twentieth century. They reflect in microcosm how those communities reacted to changes in working practices, the decline of paternalist small mills and increased competition from more efficient and larger international paper conglomerates. Their stories, while inevitably telling of an industry that exists no longer along the Water of Leith, are at times humorous, moving and instructive. They are about communities and individuals at work and at play, and about lives lived out in service to what was once a major industrial force in Edinburgh and Scotland.

Biographies

JIM WHITE
Jim White was born in 1949. He attended Murrayfield Primary and Forrester Secondary schools before going to work in the mill of John Galloway & Sons straight from school. He started work as a trainee technician in March 1965, when he spent about a month in each department following the natural progression of the processes through the mill. In September 1968 he left the mill and is currently working for Scotsman Publications Ltd.

KATE MILNE
Kate Milne (née Conaboy) was born in Perth in 1938. She attended Perth Academy and subsequently trained in nursing at the Edinburgh Royal Infirmary. Prior to taking up a post at the mill of John Galloway & Sons, she worked at the Elsie Inglis Maternity Hospital. In 1958 she became the first nurse and welfare officer at the Galloway Mill. She left the mill in 1965 to start a family.

NAN AITKEN
Nan Aitken was born in Edinburgh in 1916. She attended Juniper Green Higher Grade School before starting work in the papermaking industry in 1930. She began work in the cutter house at the Kinleith Mill of Henry Bruce & Sons

and subsequently transferred to the salle at Kinleith until the mill's closure in 1966. Between 1966 and 1975 she worked at Waddies Printers, Edinburgh.

'MARY REID'*
'Mary Reid' was born in Edinburgh in 1923. In 1937, at the age of fourteen, she followed a family tradition started by her grandfather and father and went to work at the Kinleith Mill of Henry Bruce & Sons. She began work in the cutter house and then moved to the salle. Although she took a break in employment between 1941 and 1955, she returned to the mill and worked in the salle for a further eleven years until Kinleith closed in 1966. After its closure she worked at Waddies Printers, Edinburgh.

THALLON VEITCH
Thallon Veitch was born in Edinburgh in 1927. He attended Balerno Primary and Currie Senior schools. From school he went to work briefly at Charles Spinks, Sawmill and Wood Turners, before starting work at the Balerno Bank Mill of John Galloway & Sons in 1942. He began work in the machine house at the Galloway Mill, but after an accident he transferred to the salle. He was promoted to the position of head finisher and remained at John Galloway & Sons until 1972 as, after the mill closed, he was in charge of clearing out remaining paper stocks. On leaving the Galloway Mill, he continued to work in the papermaking industry with Grosvenor Chatter and Hawarden Sheeters.

RICHARD BLAIKIE
Richard Blaikie was born in Edinburgh in 1938. He was educated at Currie Junior and Secondary schools. After leaving full-time education, he was employed at East Kin-

BIOGRAPHIES

leith Farm before starting work at Woodhall Mill in 1957. His first position at the mill was as a 'kepper boy', but he trained in many areas of the mill before becoming a shift supervisor. Mr Blaikie continued to work at Woodhall until its closure in 1984. He was then employed firstly at the Granton Works of British Gas and secondly at Currie Community High School before taking early retirement at the age of sixty-two.

WILLIAM NELSON

William Nelson was born in 1921 in Edinburgh and attended Bruntsfield Primary and George Heriot's schools. He trained as an accountant and worked for Edinburgh Corporation Transport between 1939 and 1948. In 1948 he joined John Galloway & Sons as a bookkeeper. He worked there until 1956 when he moved to Caldwell's Mill in Inverkeithing in Fife to become company secretary. His career continued as company secretary of Saddlers Transport Ltd; he subsequently lectured in accountancy at Kirkcaldy College of Technology.

* Please note that 'Mary Reid' is a pseudonym that we have used at the request of the interviewee.

Jim White

I WENT to what's now Forrester High in Broomhouse Road in Edinburgh. And I left there in the early days of 1965. I was on a course leading to higher education and university but I really didn't like school and I was very anxious to get out. I was able to leave school because I was over fifteen at the time. And I was encouraged to go and see the youth employment agency who were sort of the labour exchange, and it was there for under-eighteens. And that was normally the route to go for careers guidance, etc. And I went there in the early days of 1965 and got an old fella who went through the various cards with me and looked at the sort of jobs that were available. Most of my friends were staying on at school but one of them had already left and got a job for the princely sum of £3 10s a week, which was as a laboratory technician, and was a reasonable, maybe average, wage at the time. And this old fella went through the cards and he had wire tech at £3 10 (I was quite interested), and he had another one at £2 10, and he had one working with a surveyor holding the pole for £2 10 or £3. And then he came up with one: 'Here's one for a papermill and it's two and eightpence and a farthing an hour', and my mental arithmetic was always pretty good. And I said, 'Eh, stop that's over a fiver.' And he said 'Yeah that's what it would be.' And he's going on trying to persuade me to take the job, or to be interested in the job, telling me that this was a good opportunity, it was a training opportunity and that I could end up a papermaker. And I remember his words were, 'And you really would be somebody if you got a job as a papermaker, or you became a papermaker.' I was still sitting there saying, 'But that's five pounds, three and sixpence' or whatever it was.

So I got the card from him and made whatever arrangements there were. And I went to John Galloways Mill at Balerno to see the industrial engineer, who was a man called George Scott, who I gather had been a professional golfer in his time but that's going by the by. And got the interview, which most of us later called the 'When can you start, son?' interview. Because being 1965 it was still very much full employment, probably at the very best at that point of time in the mid-'60s. And really the employers were as anxious to get employees as people were to get jobs. So I got the job. Now I understood later there had been previously a trainee scheme, but I think possibly one or two fellows on that had lasted a year or two and had moved off on to other things. So this was them restarting the trainee scheme.

Apprenticeship

I started on the 22nd March 1965, and approximately four weeks later the second trainee started. My pay number was 2B, because I think they put the apprentices and trainees on B numbers. And every week we queued up to receive our pay. And you had to give your number, and you would fish out the paypacket from the envelope. And every week I said 2B and he [Thallon Veitch] would look, take out my packet and say 'Or not to be, lad' and hand me the packet. I think 1B was Davie Doig, who was from the previous scheme. But I was the first on this particular round. Definitely the next trainee to come in was a guy called Dick Gaughan, who later went on to become a folk singer. And the next people – and I think I've got the order right here – David Mullan was on after him and then Dennis Dingle. And then there were four of us. And we four basically chummed around together but also we went off to do the day release for the City and Guilds course. Which, having said I started in March, we didn't actually start until August of that year. But basically, I was sort of in the van and moved from one department to another. We started off, I did four weeks in the grass boiler. And then, after four weeks, when Dick Gaughan started, I moved into the next department, and so on. Four weeks later David Mullan started – he started in the grass boilers. Dick Gaughan moved on one, I moved on one and then when Dennis started we all moved on one again. So, basically we then sort of followed each other around. Well, they all followed me around, and then the other two followed Dick. But basically we went in rotation, starting off at the grass boilers and that was really the starting point.

Working the Grass Boilers

As far as the grass boilers went, I was taken there by George Scott's assistant on the first morning I started, a fellow called Ronnie Foy. And he took me up round a sort of winding lane, which I was to become very familiar with, up a sort of metal staircase to a metal floor that was quite warm. And the reason that this was warm was because of the boilers, you know this was sort of on top of the boilers, if you like. The stairs led up from the bottom of the boilers to the top of the boilers.

There were three shifts and four men on each shift, twelve in total, four at any given time. There was a boilerman who would be in charge, and an assistant boilerman and then two others, who were probably second and third assistants then, because they did call people by those names in those days. The shift I started on the first morning, the guys were known as the four Willies because they were all called Willie. This is not unusual going back to those days. And remember most of these guys who were working then – I don't think retirement was taken at sixty-five then – there was quite a few of them would go on to seventy plus. And I don't know how old these guys were but they always struck me as being quite old. And the four Willies were four very nice old men. But they were almost like four separate units; they didn't seem to have a lot of communicating. But, I mean, in their very actions. Very old-fashioned, probably they'd really sort of been around since between the war years. And they had their own ways and everybody understood what they were doing.

But they were all very kind and there were two other shifts. I remember some of the fellas on them: there was one fellow called Dod Hendry who was a particularly nice fellow; Alex Arbuckle, Pat MacErlain and an old guy called Jock Marshall who was the boilerman on one of the other shifts. And he was always pretty good to me and let me get really involved. And really what happened, and to my shame I don't remember exactly all the details, when they started putting on a boiler the second and third assistants would go through to the big warehouse you would call it, vast room if you like, where the esparto grass was continually brought in and piled up. And they would break open the bales of esparto grass and start pitchforking it onto a conveyor belt.

Sadly, I didn't ever see this but there was supposed to be one afternoon when they found a lizard amongst the esparto grass. But whether or not, people went away and fought in the war in those days but they didn't necessarily go on holidays to the sort of tropical places so whether it was the sort of lizard that you see, the tiny wee things or whether it was the bigger kind that you find in the Canaries, I don't know. But they claim that they found a lizard in the esparto grass.

Anyway, they used to pitchfork this onto a conveyor belt and the conveyor belt would run along and above the boilers and when they were filling a boiler they would have a chute that would take the grass down into that boiler. And the assistant boilerman had the one wonderful job of just basically pitchforking the stuff in to make sure it didn't miss the hole from the top of the boiler and you got that in there. And basically as I understand it there was caustic soda[1] in the boiler, and when the boiler was full the lid went on and it was screwed down under pressure and it was left to boil, like cooking I suppose.

Going up the stairs, the height of the stairs was the height of the boilers, so I'm guessing it would be about 20 feet. Across the way, 18 feet maybe, or thereabouts. But when they came to be opened, when the boilermen were satisfied they were ready, we would take the locks off them. Basically, they were bolted down. And over each boiler there was a sort of pipe in almost a u-bend turn, so it was pointing down into the boiler. And when the lid was removed a nozzle would then be put across this pipe and it basically put on a high jet stream of water. You could look down into the boiler when the lid was back off and the steam had gone – it was almost like a cake, although it was sort of indented rather than risen at the top. But it looked for all the world like a cake, and then they put on the jet stream of water and you would aim this in and basically force with water so that what was in this boiler would run away. And that carried it away to the potchers. That was how it was done by the boilerman in particular; I was saying it was Jock Marshall, the one who was always quite happy to let me have a shot. I mean I loved standing there, sort of leaning over this boiler pointing the hose down and washing all the stuff away and that was it, that was basically the grass boilers.

To a great extent there was almost no need for supervision. People just got on with it, and I think there was a foreman who naturally spent most of his time down at the very end process at the paper machine. And I can't really think of many times I ever seen the foreman up at the grass boilers. I did see the manager up there, the mill manager who often had the title 'the papermaker'. The mill manager was a fellow called Alex Izzat. And you wouldn't see him very often up in the grass boilers, but you'd see him more often than you'd see the foreman. There were three shift foremen. Later on, one of those shift foremen became a sort of senior foreman and worked day shift. So he was almost like an assistant manager.

The Potchers

What then happened was this 'stuff' as they used to call it flowed away and went towards the potchers. By this time it was a sort of a porridgy substance, only it was brown and it was that sort of mix. Didn't particularly look very nice. It went round in a drum and some moisture was taken off it. But also at this stage there was recycling of paper, known as broke. This recycled paper came from the paper machine where the process had broken the paper. Maybe a tear had happened in the paper mill and this could be relatively damp paper that would be taken away for repulping. There was also the paper at the cutting stage. Maybe ends of paper and stuff like that. Pretty hard paper but really quite papery by that time, that was another lot that came in. And this was put in amongst this 'stuff' at this juncture to basically be recycled and broken up.

And there were two chutes which went over one of the lanes that you went up to get to the grass boilers. One of them was a big high chute, a very wide chute, where the paper came down from the salle, which was where the women looked at the paper and picked out the stuff that had the various faults in it. And the other was a smaller chute, which came down from the guillotine room, and that paper went down there. It was mainly more like shavings and not particularly big bits. But the stuff that came up from where the salle was, you know, full-size paper that was ready to go out but failed the quality control, if you like. They came down chutes into barrows. If somebody was a bit reckless without whistling first to say there's paper on its way, the barrow would go shooting across because the very force of the paper would throw it across the floor.

But we used to have fellas who would carry the other paper up from the machines and would come back and do it; they were called broke boys. At the potchers there was just one man in charge for each shift. The most famous of the lot was a guy called Jimmy Lawson who I think had been a Desert Rat and he was a total character. He was the sort of fellow who really had the best interests of the mill at heart. But he must have been a thorn in the flesh of the manager, because he chased all over the place. 'You're putting too much broke into here, Mr Izzat.'[2] And he used to come and say to me and say to anybody who's around, 'Oh, there's too much of this stuff going in; it's all going to go wrong.' But, that was basically the potchers.

The Towers

The next place where I went after I was discharged from the potchers was the towers. The last thing in the process was where the paper, where the 'stuff' at that time as it was called, was bleached. Occasionally we'd put in some wood chip, sort of pulp boards, I think they came in from Sweden. And they would get put in there. And then the bleach would be put in, so it was white. It would then go to an area called the towers, where it would settle for a while. And it would be left just to settle down, let any fumes come off, having just been bleached. I don't remember too much about the towers – there was really very little done. They had three guys who were towermen but I don't know what they ever did. It was a fairly light job, I would imagine.

Presspâté

So the next place that the 'stuff' went to was called the presspâté, and this was basically a sort of place with stone baffles. The idea was that anything that was in amongst this, like foreign bodies, metal or anything like that, would come out. And then it went across – it always reminds me of someplace in the fairground – it went across something that shook very much. It had a metal part at the bottom and basically this was to take out any other impurities, like wee bits of wood or anything like that. And generally the presspâtés were a sort of cleaning process and very rough and ready, very old-fashioned, very low-tech.

I remember three fellas there very well. One was called Tiny Rankin, a smashing fella, I think he was about seventy-odds at the time. Another was called Tam McNeil and another was called Willie Stoddart. I remember Willie Stoddart well because most of the guys at that time drank their tea from large tins of, what was it, Lyons Gold Star Bank Syrup it was. So they would basically cut the top off the tin and then they would put a handle on it and they would have a big tin mug, if you like, for drinking out of. And this tin when the tea was hot could be swung back and forwards with the handle so that it cooled down.

JIM WHITE

Willie Stoddart, like many of them, had a little pack that they brought to work that had tea in one end and sugar in the other. It was a little sort of tin thing and it separated the tea from the sugar. But they always had very stiff little lids on them and Willie Stoddart one day asked me to make his tea, and I had a devil of a fight with the lid to get it off. And when it did come off I think half of the tea went across the floor. I think he got his tea and he didn't say a word, but two or three days later Tiny on one of the other shifts, 'Aye,' he says, 'Willie will no be asking you to make his tea again.' So no, I didn't really have a reputation for making tea either. But that was the presspâté.

The Beaters

From there the stuff went to the beaters, so I moved on to the beaters, where there were two men per shift. And basically the beaterman was actually one of the best-paid guys in the mill, 'cause it was a fairly important job. Although it was maybe down to a touch of skill and a touch of almost anti-science – it was more of a kind of art than anything else. The stuff went in there and it was really intended to be beaten down to the pulp – from lumpy porridge we were getting down towards almost like semolina so that it would just flow. After it went through this process it was ready to go to the paper machine.

Now having done the training through all those departments, I then moved off and went back to the sort of the periphery processes. In general terms, because everyone came in about four weeks after each other, we were roughly four weeks in most places. And I think there might have been from time to time somebody forgot to arrange us to move and we didn't know where we were going to move next. In general terms I would say I was four weeks in the grass boilers, four weeks in the potchers, four weeks in the presspâté, four weeks in the beaters.

Caustic Soda
Oh, I tell a lie. In actual fact, I came to the beaters later. It was after the presspâté I went off to work in the periphery and then I came back to the beaters. But the periphery stuff that I went to work in was where they did the caustic soda. To be honest, to this day I still don't know too much about it. I don't know how much these guys knew about it either. It was tanks where we made the caustic soda. I think I had four weeks out, because it was summertime at that point in time. I remember one of the fellows in particular – a guy called Willie Paul – who spent his entire life working out how he would do that day's bet. From there I think I spent a couple of days round as part of the four weeks with this other Henry Hall fellow, who again was involved in doing stuff for caustic soda. To this day, I think that part of the training was totally lost on me.

The Gundy House
Then after that I went to what was known, and don't ask me why, as the gundy house, which was where they basically slaked the lime, which I think was used for the bleach that went in the potchers. And for some reason that was just a two-man job – it was a one-man job, but it was done on two shifts. I think they only needed so much, so they were able to produce enough for the mill off two shifts. Working in that place I used to frequently go home with white hair; the dust off the lime went everywhere. It basically was shovelling lime into a slaker, and off it went and became whatever and that was that. And those particular departments, they was almost like a wee rest. I wouldn't say shovelling lime was a rest, but they were away from the process.

JIM WHITE

COATING PLANT AND PAPER MACHINES

Then I went off and did one other sort of periphery department which was the coating plant, where we basically made the coating for the paper. It was the coating that went to give the high finish to the Galloways papers. The Galloways papers were galart and galitho. So I worked there for a wee while and then I went onto the machines. And there were two paper machines at Galloways, very often referred to as the big side and the wee side. But the real truth about it was the one was a much faster machine which made paper, which made *real paper*, and the other one made what was often described as boards but really was laminated paper. It was a bit thicker. The paper machine mainly made paper for magazines – the people we made paper for were George Newnes, who produced a magazine called *Country Life*. And also John Moores for the Littlewoods catalogues. I'm sure there were others, too, but I mean those were the two famous names that we made paper for.

On the other side, the other machine, in general terms through the week it was gala boards as they were called and galitho boards. They were mainly covers for magazines or slightly bigger than magazines, but certainly not for covers of books or anything like that. The other thing that would be done on the Number 1 machine on a Friday night was colour index boards. These are the little things for index cards that you see in old-fashioned filing systems. Because the mill always worked to a Saturday twelve o'clock, the colours were done Friday night over to Saturday morning so that the whole thing could be cleaned out and all the colour would be away and we'd start up on the whites again on a Sunday night. That was always fun and games because you could just get a couple of hours rest while the struggle was to try and get to salmon, which was always a very difficult thing to try and get the colour right. And while they were running the colours to get it right, off would go the broke boys with more and more stuff that just wasn't quite right. You know, the stuff that was blue instead of salmon and so on. But that was always a wee bit of a problem.

I think probably people saw the faster machine as being the big machine, but whether or not, they preferred to work on it for no other reason than it would seem the more senior one. Because usually there was a sort of pecking order. The machine man on the bigger machine – known as the Number 2 machine – would be senior, or would be considered senior to the machineman on the wee side or the Number 1 machine. Although it was the wee side, it was actually the board machine, which was a bigger machine but it went slower.

So to a certain extent, if I remember rightly, if you were a machineman on the Number 1 machine and you'd been there the longest, and someone left on the Number 2 machine you would get promoted across to the Number 2 machine. Whether there was any more money in it, I don't think there was. I think it was purely a pecking-order thing. And I don't necessarily think the top machineman on the Number 2 would have got the foreman's job the next time around, 'cause I think there was one guy I remember getting promoted to a foreman came off the Number 1 machine.

But there were three machinemen – well, there was a machineman on each shift. So if you take each shift, on the Number 2 machine there was a machineman and an assistant, who was often known as the drier man because he worked primarily at the dry end. There was definitely a wireman on the Number 1 machine but whether or not he covered both machines, I can't remember. Then there was the second and third assistants at the dry end – that was their official title, but they were known as broke boys because it was their job when the paper broke to jump into the pit below where the paper ran, and first of all get the paper back running again, and secondly, gather up the stuff and take it out.

So what was happening here was the 'stuff', or the pulp by this time as it was almost was, would flow down onto a wire and on this wire it was almost a draining thing. It would be almost formed by the time it left the wire. I don't know how long the wire would be, but maybe, I don't know, 30, 40 feet long. On the Number 2 machine it was a single wire. On the Number 1 machine there were two wires, one a good bit above the other one. And here you'd effectively have two sheets of paper joining each other, being laminated and going off down the paper machine.

Felts

The wires used to come from United Wireworks, which were at Granton. And under the wires there would be a felt and the felts would basically last, I don't know, probably a couple of weeks or so. And they would get changed over on a Saturday morning. There was a queue for them because people would say, 'Ah, we're getting a new carpet delivered,' and alright you're next in line for the felt. So the felt would come off the machine and it would be going under the carpet in somebody's house. And to be honest I would imagine it would need a good bit of cleaning up.

Paper Reels

So anyway the paper would come across there and it would go through various rollers, which were very, very hot and that's where there was a danger of the paper breaking. It would go round these rollers, which were basically full of steam, dry the paper off until it became real paper and it got to a reel at the end. And it was reeled on and on and on until I think probably the average reel would weigh about a ton by the time we took it off.

And that was a process. There were two spindles at the end of this machine, so that when they got a reel full they would break the paper and get it on to the next spindle. In the main, we were working in those days with electrical block and tackles. There were some places in the mill where I think we still had to use the old chains and pull them up. But it was an electrical block and tackle that would have taken that away onto a barrow and on to the next process. That was basically where the paper came to an end as far as the process to being paper.

There was a scale there for weighing the paper, and obviously they had allowances made for the weight of the shell that the paper was going round, and the barrow and such. But the scale was also used by the broke boys, because they would have games with who could carry the most. The hard paper, I mean if it had really been through the driers or it came from a further process further down, it would be very, very heavy and it would cut into your shoulders. But the half-damp stuff you could pile up and pile up and pile up, and the weight would be there and it would be absolutely massive. And the problem was getting it through the doors. But it didn't cut into you the same; it was purely a matter of weight.

They'd carry it on their shoulders, and some of these guys weren't particularly big, and you would be walking through the mill and you'd suddenly come across this guy going up the stairs and you'd see he'd be like a speck with this big mountain on top of him. And I would say I've seen them maybe 5 or 6 feet across in diameter. I mean, if the guy did it for too long it was bound to do some damage to his neck, because they were sort of up over on the shoulder and the neck, and the paper way up in the air.

And they used to have a game where they would stand on the scales so they were weighed – so, right, that's whatever, 9 stone, 10 stone, off they go, then they would come back with the load and they'd weigh them and it was who could carry the most. I think it was more esteem than anything else. I think the record was something like 10 stone he carried, it might have been a lot more, I don't really remember. But there was a fella who was known as Muscles. I think he was called George Martin, I could be wrong, but his other nickname was Wee Craw, 'cause there was already a Big Craw and this Wee Craw was Craw's nephew. There were two families in the Main in Balerno at the time: the Martins and the Swans. And he was one of the Martins, there were stacks of them. And as I say, one of them had the nickname Craw and this was his nephew, Wee Craw, but he was also known as Muscles because I think he did actually hold the record for carrying the most.

Damping Process and the Calenders

After the paper came off the paper machine, it went to a machine called the damper. Which basically meant that the paper which had just been nicely dried was given a surface of damping. And the real reason is the paper had to be dried so that it would actually get all the moisture out and become firm and together; this was the damping process. It was almost like the first stage of spit and polishing, because the next stage was the super-calender. And the super-calender was basically a tower of rollers, and the paper would go in and out and in and out and in and out and be shined up. And this would give the paper its shiny look. The calenders had two guys on them, and there was one guy on the damper and they worked as a team. We had a Number 1 calender that covered the Number 1 paper machine, and the Number 2 calender covered the Number 2 paper machine. The Number 3 calender, I never quite figured out what the devil we did with that because it was only working one shift. They only came in and worked 7 till 3.

There was also a couple of other machines. The conditioner, which I think we only used when the papermaker would look at it and say there's certain paper needing conditioned. It was run round very old-fashioned rollers, which were wooden slats round a roller, so this machine made an awful lot of noise. It wasn't considered a particularly major job, because quite often guys who had been effectively broke boys one minute would be given the job of runner of the conditioner the next. And that was running the whole thing, so it wasn't considered a major responsibility and it was more like giving the paper an airing.

There was another job that I was involved in for a wee while with a guy called Dougie Wilson. He used to do it on day shift, and this was called the winder. Basically, any paper that was thought not to be wound on tightly enough would be wound through this to tighten it up. And then the paper went off to the cutters. And again there was a Number 1 cutter for the bigger, bulkier paper, and the Number 2 cutter for the faster paper. And in here the paper would be cut to the sizes.

The width of the paper on the reel was known as the deckle. Let's say we wanted three sheets of paper across the way, 25 inches. The deckle might be fixed at 79 inches, so there'd be an inch each side and an inch between the sheets. So they would go to the cutters and you'd have all the stuff trimmed off at the side and in-between. And you would have sheets of paper coming out that would be 25 by whatever they were the other way round, and they would then be shipped off to the salle.

WATER TREATMENT PLANT
The one place I didn't ever cover in the peripheries was the water treatment plant, and that did just seem like a home from home. I don't know what happened there; I think these fellas went for a walk every couple of hours and said, 'Oh ah, looks fine', and away they went. That's probably very unfair, but they didn't ever really seem to be terribly overstretched. I think it was more a case of it was almost like a bailiff than anything else.

PAPER TESTING
I went into the paper testing. Paper testing was an ongoing process with two people per shift, the paper tester and the assistant paper tester. They had a proper lab across as a separate block, where they had the technical manager – a fella called Jack Jones. The chemist was a fella called David Donald. And then there were about three or four young lads who were just basically technicians. They used to go around testing things like the caustic soda, and I'm sure they used to do other things as well.

Basically, the paper tester's job was to do a full test on the first reel of any new order. In fact, he did a full sample test when basically the paper was ready to move to this new order, and then there was smaller tests done throughout the order. If it was a long order, maybe over thirty reels or something like that, you'd do a full test every couple of hours. Because I think, in actual fact, effectively a roll came off the Number 2 machine every forty minutes. And a reel came off the Number 1 machine every hour, or thereabouts.

For a full test we'd get a piece off the roll, the full width of the reel. And it would be in length probably about 4 feet. And we had our own table in the labs, so when we got there we put it on the table and we trimmed it so that it was exactly the size of the table. And then there were grooves in the table where we could cut the paper with a Stanley knife very precisely. Then we would take one part of the paper, and we had a template. And from that template we would tear the surplus paper so we had four sheets exactly the same size. And we had scales, which we used to check the weight of the paper. So effectively we had four sheets, one from the left – inside left, if you like – inside right, right centre, and the right. We would take a bit from each of them and we would mark down what each of them weighed.

The weight of paper in those days, it changed; I think it was about 1968 it changed. It changed over to the way it's done now, grams per square metre. Before that, every paper manufacturer had their own weight of paper, and Galloways was demy-four-eighties. I can't be totally definite about this, but I think demy was 23 by 17, something like that. And effectively you would quote the weight. I always remember George Newnes and his *Country Life* was 26 pounds demy-four-eighties. That meant that 480 sheets of that size – which I think was 23 by 17, as I say – would weigh 26 pounds. And obviously the scales we had were adjusted, and the template we had was adjusted, so that it made it easy. But the gsm[3] for 26 turned out to be 83, if I remember rightly.

So that was one exercise. The next exercise was another part of the paper which was taken again over the full width of the reel just on the middle slat. We put it into a machine which basically measured the bulk of it, and this was the nearest we got to high-tech. It would draw a graph electronically of the paper that had gone through. So that would be test number two.

Number three, we only did a full test on a very narrow strip, but we did various things with this. The first thing would be what was known as a calliper test – sometimes known as bulk – where you would basically put it through a machine and it's effectively looking at the thickness. So you would take ten readings across the width and you would record those. And then the same piece of paper we would use for the burst test, which was basically pumping up to see at what level and pressure it would actually burst the paper, and you'd do that across the width of the reel. And then the remaining strip of paper across the width, you would use some of these bits for every test, some of the bits in others.

One bit used for every test was the loading test, where you took a gram of paper and you rolled it up and stuck it in an incinerator, and at the end when it was finally burned you would empty out the ash. And you'd weigh the ash and that would tell you what percentage of loading there was in the paper. In other words, what percentage of china clay could be in it, part of the coating that would come out in the ash. The more you put in the mix the higher that would be. If I remember rightly, 24 per cent was about the sort of norm.

Another test we did was the wax test. We heated waxes which had different strengths. It was similar to what they used to put on a sealing wax on parcels, and round the string. They were tall waxes that we would have heated so that the pressure would go on to the paper. We would leave them there, and when they cooled we would pull them away. And at the end of the day you'd look for the first one of the series – let's say there was there was a Number 6 wax, a Number 7 wax, a Number 8 wax, a Number 9, 10 and so on. You'd have a rough idea where you were starting from. So that you should be able to say – right, Number 6 lifted no blister, Number 7 lifted no blister, and Number 8 blistered. Basically, at what stage does the surface rip when you pull something off it. So you know if you pulled it off and Number 6 was a problem, then you'd be cursing because you should have put 4 and 5 on, because you'd have to start all over again. But in general terms you knew roughly where you were.

There was also an oil test, which was basically a drip of oil in a wee sort of roller that rolled across the paper. You had a wee stop-clock there, and you were looking for how long it took to absorb the oil you put. There was another test where it was done with a stethoscope. We were testing for smoothness and how this thing worked; I mean it was electronic equipment, but how it quite measured the smoothness I'm blowed if I know. But somebody thought it did.

And then there was the final bit which some people put as more important than any other – the IGT test. I gathered it was something that came from Holland, and it was basically a printing test to decide at what stage the paper would rip away from itself when pressurised. And there was two mechanisms, one for the more likely paper to tear – which was a very slow arm test which it just sort of rocked through – and the other a spring test that ripped right through. And you had certain levels which the paper had to achieve, and you knew if ever the paper ripped a good bit earlier than it should have done there was all hell to pay. Everybody was going around getting very worried.

So really, that was the tests that the tester did. And the tester, although he had an assistant, the assistant did very little by way of that. But the assistants had their own job that was known as the moistures. And the idea was we would go to other machines and take samples. I worked from March until about late August doing this. On the damper job we would cut with a Stanley knife from the middle of the reel after the damping had been done. We'd cut about four deep squares of paper, and we would take a piece of paper into a moisture-testing machine. And that would tell us the percentage of moisture in the paper. I would record, obviously, what reel it was, and the result. Then we would later get a sample whilst the reel was running through the super-calender of how the moisture was then. So you'd expect a fair bit of moisture after it had been damped, and you would expect a good bit less after it had been rubbed a wee bit by the calenders. So effectively there was a record there.

How well these records were looked at is another matter. I mean, the paper tester's job was doing the full test, and one part that comes back in my mind was we came up to the foreman's office and recorded the results, and we recorded it for the machine room right actually at the machine. But we also did another job, checking under an ultraviolet to make sure that there was no sort of bad pattern in the paper.

And it was shown under an ultraviolet light. The bits we weighed we always kept as a sample within the files that we had there. So that basically people could come back and refer to all of these tests that had been done on any particular order on any particular reel.

Becoming Assistant Paper Tester

So after I'd been in the paper testing, at a later stage I went off and spent some time in the super-calenders, and in the cutting, as well as a couple of weeks in the binders. But what actually happened was when I was in the paper testing, a job came up for an assistant, and I was rather keen to do something because I realised it was coming towards the end of the mill and I was beginning to run out of places to go. And I wasn't sure what they were going to do with me. So I thought, I might as well grab the chance of doing something I quite fancy when it's here. So I took the chance to become an assistant paper tester, and I think that at that point of time there was a little bit of friction between the fellow who replaced George Scott as the industrial engineer and the man who was looking after the training scheme, a guy called Iain Richardson. And there was a little bit between them and Jack Jones at the time, because Jack Jones had been approached by me and he was quite keen to have me in the team. Iain Richardson couldn't understand why I was giving up on the three-year training scheme.

The apprenticeship was very open; you'd go round the mill. One of the jokes that people used to talk about in those days was, 'Is this the job where you go round the mill and eventually take over?' 'Cause they did sort of make out that once you've done all that, just look what you'll be. But people who'd gone halfway round before had ended up not much better than the broke boys. And I don't say that in any sort of way other than the fact that the broke boys were seen as sort of the bottom end of the market. That's where everyone came in – if you came in off the street you got a job as a broke boy. It was the bottom end of the jobs at the mill, and then maybe if you were lucky you got a chance to do something else.

The thought that you'd gone round and been a trainee, and you thought you'd learnt some skills, just to start where everybody else was starting seemed pretty pointless to me. And I think the fear was that that's where we would end up if we didn't get every chance what was going.

At this point in time I was still just sixteen and I'd been on the scheme for less than a year. I think I was about a week short of being on it for a year when I actually started the first shift. And I think on top of everything else I've already said, I went into Galloways because it paid more and here was a chance – the shift payment was even more than I was getting. So I think it was maybe up to eight or nine pounds a week. And you know, I was really quite well off compared to friends of mine that were still at school, and even friends of mine that had started other jobs. So this was good. And I don't think Iain Richardson totally appreciated it, and he said, 'Well, okay, you can help out Jack Jones until we get somebody else.' And then he finally did manage to find somebody else by the end of the summer, so I was shunted back onto the scheme. By this time Dickie had got in front of me.

Training in the Salle

So having gone back into the training scheme I was now following Dick. And when I was working in the cutters he'd moved on to the salle, where the paper was being examined. And really what Dick was doing, and what I went up there to do, was to stand and watch the girls who worked very, very quickly. It was certainly quite skilled; they could just see in an entire sheet of paper in a second. Counting was a more senior job. They started wearing green coats to show that they were still on the training. And they got a blue coat when they were probationary skilled. And they got a pink coat working on the counter. You could recognise what they were doing. There were probably about sixty or seventy women, I would guess, just imagining the number of aisles there were in the place. And they would basically pull the sheets from right to left from one pile and make another pile. And all of a sudden one would shoot over to the side. And my job was to stand there and say – right, one sheet of paper failed, why? And sometimes it was quite easy, but sometimes – you know this shows you the sort of the eye that these women had – I would be standing there saying, 'There's nothing wrong with that', and they would say, 'No, there it is' – some very minor defect they had picked up, quite incredibly. There were women who would check the paper and there was women who counted the paper.

Then we made up an analysis of the rejected paper, and George Orr dressed it up and wrote a report to the management by order and what have you. I mean the sort of the things we got were sort of shy little almost holes in the paper, usually caused by maybe a bit of wood on the drying. Sometimes we got what was known as crushed, torn and folded, which was just bits of paper that got crushed coming through the cutters and stuff like that. So there was a rejection rate; it wasn't ridiculously high, but there was a rejection rate.

MILL CRISIS
It was coming up for Christmas in '66 by this time, and I was really wondering what I was going to do next, when they had another crisis in paper testing – they lost another couple of assistants. And I went back and said to Iain Richardson, 'I'm going to go back there and this time I'll just to go back and stay, because I don't know if there's anywhere else they can send me.' And Jack Jones was quite happy to take me back, so that was it.

Because there was a real shortage I went back on the twelve-hour shifts. And there were only two of us. I remember various people said, 'Oh aye, that's ridiculous, you are only seventeen, you cannae be doing twelve-hour shifts.' Climb up chimneys and stuff like this, you know, it was really back to the dark old days. But it wasn't really. By this time the mill had just gone into a wee bit of a crisis and we had been put on what is known as short time. The mill was closed every Thursday at twelve noon.

There was a genuine lack of orders, I think, at the time. Now I think it was at this stage one of the paper testers left. So we had a situation where we only had two paper testers left, and one of them said, I really would appreciate you not taking anybody else on. Because if I get twelve-hour shifts for three and a half days, I could just make ends meet. If I go onto eight-hour days at three and a half days, I'll be skint. And the same thing happened in the assistants' section.

ON THE DOLE

The weeks when we had a full week I was getting a very good pay, and by now I'd really gone into overdrive. And the weeks when we didn't, when we were on short time, I was still making quite good pay. But I got harangued into going to the youth employment service, which is effectively the dole, the place that gave me the job. You could claim for the days that you didn't work. I remember dragging myself in there, and I got such a lecture from the old guy there who said, 'Sonny, it's up to you but with you not turning up here last week' – or whenever it was – 'you've lost two and sixpence' – because you know, you've lost the claim on that day for dole money.

But I was greatly amused at the old fellow in the youth employment who wanted me to turn up and collect my two and six, when even at that point in time my wage for three-and-a-half days was more than most of my pals would have been if they'd been in overtime, you know. It was as simple as that. I really wasn't that bothered. But I think I did take it ill at the fact that on top of everything else it was the youth employment – I felt I was a bit more grown-up than that.

I think you had to lose three days before you could start claiming days. But in fairness, I think what Galloways tried to do was, they almost anticipated short time so that they gave us short time within the sort of area that we would have otherwise have lost the rolling days. You had to go three days within thirteen weeks without anything before they would start paying you unemployment benefit. When you then got the unemployment benefit, if you didn't go unemployed again within the next thirteen weeks you would lose and you would have to start all over again. So Galloways at one stage actually gave us short time to let us continue and not lose out on the days. So that we were in a position to say, right, well, we've served your lie days, or whatever they were called, and you would get unemployment benefit on those days. And that sounds like, thank you for shooting us in the head, for putting us on short time. But given the following week they got us to work the weekend and didn't close the mill down for a fortnight we just ran right through. It meant that everybody got the real bonus of: 1) we hadn't lost the unemployment when we were hit by short time again; and 2) we'd all got the beano from having weekend working, which was all overtime: double time and time and a half. So that was quite good.

Working Hours and Holidays
The mill worked on a three-shift basis. And the whole mill started at ten o'clock on a Sunday night and finished at

noon on a Saturday. My hours initially as a trainee were 8 o'clock to 4.30, four days a week, and 8 o'clock to 4.45 on a Monday, and then 8 to 11 on a Saturday. And it was a 45-minute lunch break. Interestingly, Christmas Day in those days was not a holiday in Scotland, and we had to work Christmas Day. Although the first year I was there it was a Saturday, and I'm sure quite a few of us who were not really totally required to work managed to find some reason why we weren't well. But later on I actually worked Christmas Eve nightshift over to Christmas morning, and then came back on Christmas night, which was a bit of a drag.

A Proper Post

So anyway I did that in the mill, chunted along for a wee while, and then one Monday morning I went in and no sign of the tester. And somebody came in and said to me – you know this is coming up for starting time – 'Jim, you're to do the tester's job this morning.' And I says, 'Why?' 'Oh, Willie had an accident on Friday night. He was taken away to hospital and he's not going to be in for a week.' So I thought, no sign of an assistant, I'll just need to let that job go and we'll just get on with it.

So at eight o'clock, Alex Izzat, manager in the mill, came in and said to me, 'Son, you've got the job, you can do it, you've started now and well done.' And then he said to me, 'And I've told them you're getting paid as if you're twenty-one.' And I said, 'Damn right, do you think I'd be doing this if I wasn't?' Because they had this scale that if you weren't in a sort of fixed job like the paper tester's job, you'd be on a scale that would get paid at fifteen, sixteen, seventeen, eighteen, nineteen, twenty, and you didn't get the full whack until you were twenty-one. So that was me onto the full whack, twenty-one-year-old's pay, and by this time I was not long eighteen.

And I think I was on twelve hours for a while, because Willie didn't come back after his accident. What actually happened was a shell, a big steel thing that was the centre of each of the rolls of paper, he got in the road of it. I think he was clowning around on the night shift when there was a bit of paper and it switched over into a reel with an empty shell and somehow it went and hit him on the foot and broke his toe. So that put him out of action and put me into his job. And lo, when he came back we all went onto eight-hour shifts at that point. But for a wee while I was earning, I think it actually got up as far as £30 a week. And I was nearly getting £20 actual take-home pay. Which, as I say, I mean by this time most of my pals would be taking home four or five pound if they were lucky. So I really was sort of well off and I did enjoy living the high life on it. And basically I went on in that job from there until I left in 1968.

Day Release
I started the day release in August 1965, and the first year we were at Newbattle. I wouldn't say it was Newbattle College, it was actually Esk Valley College, but Esk Valley College had not really been built. I think there were two day release classes each week. Dick and I went to one, and David and Dennis went to the other. And in the class there was another fella called Jim Aitken, who turned out to be Scotland's Grand Slam skipper in 1984.

But we had a fella called Wright who taught us papermaking, and the technical side was a more senior man called Tom Hutchison. And that was sort of brought into us, I think it was called applied science. There was another fellow called Mr Douglas, who taught us the sort of social issues. This I think was one of these things that although it didn't come into the exam it was very much part of – if you were going to have kids on day release in the 1960s, you'll teach them a little bit about the world. We were a year at the place at Newbattle, and then we moved to another part of Esk Valley College. I think we were there for the last two years, which was down in the valley at Dalkeith. It had been St David's Primary School, very much a sort of 1920s/'30s old-fashioned school, single-storey affair. We had the exam in 1968, and the real Esk Valley College was built just in time for me to receive the certificate there in 1969, by which time I was working as a wages clerk. I had absolutely no need for it at all.

I can't honestly remember too much about the exams as we went through. I must have done enough to pass them. I remember Tom Hutchison, the applied science and the more senior lecturer, continually saying, 'Don't do the calculation. As far as we know, the calculation, if you don't get it right, you might get nothing out of twenty.' And I wasn't particularly gifted scientifically; I was far more gifted in terms of numbers. So I totally bucked the trend, I insisted on doing the calculation. And I was fairly confident that a calculation I could get right. And that was worth twenty marks, and I thought if I get thirty out of the other eighty I might pass. I don't think I passed with any great mark at all. I've got the feeling John Connor from Woodhall, he might have got distinction. But he was quite a bright fella.

I can't remember if there was anybody there from Kinleith. Kinleith used to get this reputation that all the guys there were very, very young. At Galloways I was the youngest paper tester ever. I think everybody tried to get that title, because Willie Hamill had been eighteen and a half, and Kenny Pennycook had been nineteen, and I was eighteen and a quarter. But at Kinleith there was stories of guys of seventeen getting up as far as machinemen, you know, seriously running the mill. I don't know how true that was, but I can't remember anybody from Kinleith. I remember the guys from Woodhall. I remember Jim Aitken, and there was another guy, Gerry Farrel I think his name was, from the Penicuik Mills. But one of the other things we got the benefit of is when we were at the day release, we got taken to other mills. And I do remember going to see Valleyfield in Penicuik. Polmethorn. I can't remember Esk Mills in Penicuik, but I remember going to Springfield at Lasswade. Inveresk down at Musselburgh. Strangely enough, I don't remember going to any of the other mills up the Water of Leith. I do remember going to one in Denny, the board mill. And Fettykil Mill, which recently I think had a fire, in Leslie in Fife, where they made paper bags. And those are the ones that I remember best. But those were quite good, getting out to papermills trips. We also saw a bit of the history of some of these mills as well.

And we met people. There was one fellow who came to Galloways called Bill Duncan, and I remember he showed us round Springfield Mill, then the next thing Springfield Mill closed, he was redundant and he was working for Galloways. So it was quite good we knew him when he started, because he became my boss.

I think sometimes I found what I'd learnt at work to be quite useful. I think possibly what happened was I learnt things at work and I got clarification in the sort of classroom side of it. But I think actually having a piece of paper saying I was a papermaker at the end of the day didn't really make any great difference. I don't know if Alex Izzat ever had his qualification, but I think he was the sort of fella who had a real feel for it, you know. He lived that sort of thing, and he was a good papermaker. And other guys as well, who were maybe machinemen, had pretty good knowledge of what they were doing. I don't think coming out with a certificate at nineteen necessarily helped that much.

And I doubt whether the other ones who came out with certificates have ever done very much with it, because, on top of everything else, if I remember rightly, Galloways closed at the end of '71. Which was like just over three years after I'd qualified and left the mill. And you know, what real good was it going to do them? I don't think that even if all the people that they trained had stayed we would have saved the mill.

SHOWING SCHOOL PARTIES ROUND THE MILL

Once at Galloways I seem to remember I was drafted in at the last minute. I don't know why – no one had thought about it, or whether someone else went ill – but I was asked at the end of my 7 till 2 shift if I would take a party from Balerno Primary School round the mill. And I think in the end of the day there were about three of us took a part of the party. And there were lots of jokes amongst us at the time about trailing all these kids. But I didn't realise I'd really drawn the short straw until we got into the machine room and this little boy said he was allowed to press all the buttons. And I said, 'Oh no, son, you certainly can't do that.' And he said, 'My Dad lets me press these buttons when he brings me in here on a Saturday.' And I suddenly looked and realised it was the general manager's son. So I had to keep him quiet for a wee while!

I think probably Bill Duncan showed round quite a lot of parties 'cause he'd had the experience at Springfield. I do remember another party, Bill Duncan showing a group round, and they came from what was in those days probably described as an approved school. You know, basically, not quite a borstal, but heading in that direction. And after they went away he was so shocked at their language – it was really awful, and they'd shouted things at him.

And there was one party came just to look at the paper testing and were very interested in them. I was talking about a machine where we used to run the paper through and get a sort of graph of how thick it was. I'm sure one party came just to see technical instruments. It might have been very high-tech, it was the highest-tech we had, and possibly it might have been as high-tech as quite a few places, I don't know. I think things were still relatively low-tech – I mean, we still had big barrows that we pushed around, wee wooden barrows and stuff like that. It was fairly much low-tech.

Workforce Distribution

As far as where the labour was drawn from, probably 50 per cent from Balerno. I think really if I describe it as being the shift system was 6 till 2, 2 till 10, and 10 till 6. But then the shift system for certain jobs, like myself, was 7 to 2, 2 to 10 and 10 till 7. And that hour in the morning was because those who lived outside Balerno couldn't get there before seven o'clock, or much before seven o'clock. We certainly couldn't get there for six, unless you had a car, and you can imagine not many people had a car in those days. So really, for the people who lived locally it worked out quite well. Because if a job was there – 'Right, that's a job for a local man, 'cause it's a six o'clock changeover, and that's a job for a outsider, that's seven.' A lot lived in Currie, and there were those who lived in Edinburgh. I lived in Balgreen, Edinburgh. And there were quite a lot lived sort of west side of Edinburgh, and they got over to Balerno from there. Not many would have come much further than that.

But then we had the coaches that brought people in from Whitburn, Blackburn, Bathgate. The company organised the coaches; they were Brownings, who had a place at Whitburn as well as a place in Stevenson Road in Edinburgh. I think that basically Galloways looked to the Calders and West Lothian as a place to pick up labour, because they weren't able to get enough labour locally from Currie. And remember in those days not a lot of women worked, you know. Girls would work till they got married, then they'd give up and leave. Certainly women working who had children really didn't happen. Once a woman had children that was it, she left work.

WORKING WOMEN

It was 100 per cent sexist in the '60s. They were only guys worked on the shop floor, and there were only ladies worked checking and looking at paper. The guys had the manual jobs; the women did the jobs looking at paper. There was no women on shifts. You know that would really have been totally taboo at the time.

But they worked the same hours – when I started it was 8 till 4.45, Monday; 8 till 4.30, Tuesday to Friday; and 8 till 11, Saturday. And everyday you'd have forty-five minutes for lunch, 12.30 till 1.15. And then after that we moved on to a forty-hour week, and it became something like quarter to eight in the morning till half past four at night. With forty-five minutes for lunch, and we only worked Monday to Friday. That was a big thing – a five-day week, getting out of Saturday mornings. But the mill still ran from Sunday night at ten o'clock till Saturday noon.

And the shift workers obviously got extra pay, because they worked extra hours over and above the forty-two, or forty as it became. But the women would work those set hours.

PAPERMAKING ON THE WATER OF LEITH

NICKNAMES

One of them [towermen] was called Ian Bowman, but he was always known as Willie Bauld, because there was a Hearts player just shortly before, one of the great post-war footballers called Willie Bauld, and this fella had always gone on about Willie Bauld. So he was nicknamed Willie Bauld. Just like there was another fella who always listened to Henry Hall's music – Henry Hall was a bandleader in the '30s, and he always talked about that, so he was nicknamed Henry Hall. And it took a long time to find out their real names because they were just known as Henry Hall and Willie Bauld. And Balerno was a tremendous place for having nicknames, I mean, people just weren't known by their real name.

I think there was an element of sarcasm about it, but some people used to call me Fearless. It may have been something to do with the fact that I once refused to climb a 40-feet ladder to put a bulb in. On the basis I dinnae like heights. But some people called me, that but I think that was almost an honour for somebody who didn't live in Balerno to get a nickname.

There was one thing that springs back to mind from my own angle was we often had a bit of spare time in the night shift in the paper testing area. Particularly when we were running colours and you couldn't get colours, 'cause there was nothing for us to do – they could be four hours trying to get the salmon colour. And we were sitting there one night and somebody said, 'Oh, there's such and such a horse is in that would be a terrific horse for so and so.' So at the end of the day we ended up looking through the papers, and we found something like a couple of dozen horses that all had names that related to people in the mill, and we drew up this list and then drew a little sort of bit in that was like a form guide, only it was a bit about the people. Poor old Jack Jones had a bit of limp, so we called him Hoppity. Bernie Walton was the general manager, and wherever Bernie went, within a split second you'd find Jack chasing along after him. And in the form guide, I think we had the horse for Bernie Walton was something like Right Honourable Gentleman, and the form guide read 'Hoppity on all runnings against Right Honourable Gentleman very close behind'. But dear old Fred Ainslie, who I'm sure was a really nice guy, we gave him the Snob, because he never spoke to anybody in the shop floor and said he always kept his nose in front. But to my horror, I found when I came in the next night a typed copy with it all printed up, and I got hold of George Orr and said, 'George, whatever happened to this?' And he says, 'Oh, I took it up the office and they fell about laughing.' And I said, 'But what about guys like Fred Ainslie?' He said, 'Oh, he was quite – he thought it was quite good.' And that was all that had it, I didn't want to show my face. But that was it: he had it all typed up and it was circulated all round the office. But that was I remember bits of that as being – it was only done for our amusement; it wasn't done for general publication.

In the salle was one of the great characters of Galloway's Mills: a guy called George Orr, who rejoiced in the name Pokum. And I really thought Pokum had come from the fact that he was renowned for poking people in the ribs. But then I met somebody who known him when he was about nine years old and he was called Pokum then. His father was called Dargy, and that was a nickname as well, and I don't know what Dargy meant, no idea at all. He was one of a number of guys who in the early '60s had, as old age pensioners, got together and decided they would have a sweep on who would die first. It was actually on the television news at the time, a sort of local *Scotland Today*, or whatever it was called in those days. I think the whole thing finally came to an end when one of them did die and they felt so bad about it, and that was it. But that was a renowned sort of thing.

Housing

The mill manager actually had a house right next to the premises, it was over the road from the mill, the Mill House. Yes, there was a street, which I'm sure is long since gone, which was amusingly named, and this was the proper name of it: 'Society'. But the mill houses always struck me as being pretty ropey. Having said that, I was never in any of them. But, you know, I don't think it was probably the best housing in those days. Certainly, the mill manager had what looked like quite a nice house, but he was virtually on the premises all the time, you know; he was across at his house, or he was a phone call away, or somebody running and chapping on his door.

Social Events and Annual Trips

There was a lady there called Aggie Coutts who came from Kirknewton, if I remember rightly, and she organised the trips. They were organised through Brownings, who used to have the buses that brought people in from the Calders and West Lothian. And we did have quite a few evenings out to ten pin bowling, which was relatively new at that point. There was one in Kirkcaldy, and one in Glenrothes, and one in East Kilbride at the time, and that was about it. So if you wanted to go ten pin bowling you got a coach trip, and we would go on those. But also I think we had one night near Christmas – we had a Christmas party down at Dunbar, which is only vague in my memory for good reason. And then we had a day trip to Girvan in Ayrshire on the Edinburgh Monday holiday in April. Galloways worked on local holidays. Christmas was not a local holiday.

We got trades fortnight off. Up until the last year, in 1968, when we moved to the Glasgow Fair. Glasgow Fair was very popular with quite a number of guys, because it was known as the Scottish Racing Circuit. So if you didn't go away for your holidays, during the Glasgow Fair Holidays you could have two days at Hamilton, two days at Lanark races, two days at Musselburgh, two days at Ayr, and so on and so on. You'd have an entire fortnight's holiday going to the races. But it was certainly trades to start with.

We had three days at New Year – nothing at Christmas – three days at New Year and the Edinburgh Holidays in April and September, and I think that was probably about it. Because there wasn't all the things they have today. When we had the Girvan trip, that was on the Edinburgh Monday holiday in '68. Every time I hear that song 'Daytrip to Bangor' – you know probably the one I mean – it was very much like that. I'm sure we managed to do it for under a pound.

The company put no money into it at all; it was totally unofficial. As I say, the woman who ran that was Aggie Coutts. But the best one of all was we went to Blackpool for the September weekend, and I'm certain that we each paid £6 17 6. And for that we got the coach down from Edinburgh on the Friday night and deposited back on the Monday night, and four meals a day and hotel accommodation. And the hotel accommodation, there was five of us to a room. And I think I won the toss to not end up on the zed bed. It was pretty bad. But you know, that was it, and I think you've got to look at it that's how people lived at that point in time. Towards the end of my time at Galloways, people were starting to talk about going to Spain. Before then Blackpool was, you know, you were lucky if you got there.

We used to have guys who would work the trades holidays, 'cause the trades holidays they took as the time for maintenance. Because the mill, basically it got shut down at twelve o'clock on a Saturday until ten o'clock on a Sunday night, and it was cleaned up before it was left. The last few hours on a Saturday morning, when the hoses came out, any colours, any dyes would be out of the system and that sort of stuff. But other than that the place was never looked at. So for a fortnight the whole place was dead, and engineers would work.

Unions

I was a member of the union. It was SOGAT. The union was fairly ineffectual. I think everybody knew they wouldn't go on strike. I don't think there was ever any work-to-rule or anything like that at all. I remember once – now to this day I cannot remember if I ever got satisfied that I was wrong, or that I was right for that matter – but I remember once working out that I thought we were underpaid on the number of hours we were paid. And I recall going up, and somehow or other I must have said something to somebody, and I ended up . . . not the union, I ended up going and arguing and the union couldn't understand me. And I went up and argued it out with Doris Gill. I don't think she could understand me, and we ended up disagreeing but not getting any more money. But in the union were a lot of good, genuine guys, but I think they appreciated they couldn't necessarily get any further than we were getting. They probably knew like everyone else that it was only a matter of time. But in general terms it was all pretty amicable.

JIM WHITE

HEALTH AND SAFETY
Coming back to mind, I don't remember any serious accidents. Now that's just because I can't remember. A nurse was there, and a doctor would be brought in to give you a medical. The nurse was there on a full-time day shift. Her office was in the salle beside the women, so no doubt she'd give health advice there. But she wasn't seen an awful lot about the shop floor. Probably most of the accidents would be small ones and would happen at night. I had two accidents, neither of which did me any great harm. I fell down off a few bags of casein in the coating plant and I staved my arm, but it just got bandaged up and I was away again.

There was a no-smoking policy in a lot of the areas. In a lot of the areas it wasn't totally observed. As one of the fellows sitting in the grass boilers said, 'If you want a smoke son, you just watch the stairs.' That was the nearest there was to any safety thing. I mean, I'm sure if there was an accident there, it would have been investigated and reported. But wee things, like the second accident – I cut my thumb open with a knife in, of all areas, the paper testing room, when I was trying to get wax off the wick of the candle that we lit the candles with. That was relatively bad, but it didn't put me off work. But nobody bothered. There wasn't any great thing, and certainly any idea that anybody would sue the company for anything that happened just wasn't really on.

WORK STUDY AND THE INDUSTRIAL RELATIONS ACT
Work study was the industrial engineer, and that would have been Iain Richardson latterly and George Scott to start with. The only times that I ever really saw them was

when we went for our Friday session and discussion and training. When it started off, I went up myself to see George Scott and then I went with Dick. And then I think all four of us used to go to see Iain Richardson at the same time. Fifteen minutes. 'You doing okay, son? Where are you now, oh, right, who are you working with? Henry Hall? Oh aye, right.' And that was it. I recall somebody saying the great thing about going to see Iain Richardson was he'd pass round his Capstan Full Strength, which was quite a treat.

In fairness, probably in those days that was as much as you would get anywhere. The rules weren't quite the same. The Industrial Relations Act was in 1971, so it was a good few years after I was there. And in general most of it was fairly amicable, and most of the workforce were amicable amongst each other. Yet there were times when there was disputes and wee argy-bargies, but nothing in particular. In general, it was a very good place. I'd have to say the locals in the place were pretty generous in their sort of openness with the other people as well. I mean, I always felt part of the family there. And you know, it was a pretty good place to work. And you know, compared to modern-day backstabbings, it was good.

Closing the Mills

To be honest, I don't remember too much of Kinleith closing. But certainly I think there was a feeling that things weren't going well and that it could close for lack of orders. You know Jimmy Lawson – to go back to the guy in the potchers, who was the guy who was always complaining about the broke paper – he was always coming and looking at the orders because, you know, there was always a running list of what was to be done today or tonight. 'Oh, stock again, oh, stocks, where's all this stock going?' Of course, we did make make paper for stock, when we knew that if we made 26 galart that George Newnes would come along and take it out of stock quite happily. But there was always this belief that if we were making paper for stock there was no customers, nobody buying. I think there were many, many other problems. Amongst problems towards the end – they brought in a coating machine which was going to run at something like, seventeen hundred feet a minute, or twenty-five hundred feet a minute or something like that. And that was just one failure after another. And those were supposed to be the saving graces.

Jimmy Lawson, famous potcher man, he was a guy who was always saying, 'This place is finished, this is no long to go, the doors will be closed.' And I think in general terms there was that feeling. Some people thought it was over the top, but other people knew. He was always going on about how we were making paper for stock. Things weren't good. We knew the industry was on its way out. I think the general thing was that in Edinburgh, it was a city of papermaking and publishing. Edinburgh was publishing . . . and the surrounding area, Midlothian, was basically the papermaking. That was my best recollections.

Notes

1. Caustic soda was added to esparto grass while it was in the boilers to break down the grass fibres into cellulose.
2. It was not a good idea to put too much broke into the mix, as the fibres would be broken down too much.
3. Grams per square metre.

Kate Milne

I TRAINED in nursing at the Royal [Infirmary] here in Edinburgh. I'd come from Perth and went to Edinburgh Royal and did my general training there, and then went to do midwifery. From there I went into industrial nursing at Galloways. I was going to be getting married in two or three years' time and I wanted something where I could relate with people who came into hospital and who were working. And I found the advert in one of these employment bureaus. And I applied, and then I found out it was Freddie Ainslie whose wife was a patient of mine at Elsie Inglis, so that was the tie-up.[1]

Things were starting to then get more regimented by the Health and Safety in factories. So I think that was when it started to kick in that it was easier and better to have somebody on site to do these bits and pieces, and access wasn't easy because Balerno had a bus, end of story, and there was nothing else.[2] It was quite far-thinking. I think it was probably Freddie Ainslie who instigated it all. And it is a good idea to know both sides of the person who has been injured or in hospital, what happens in the other half of their life, really.

THE JOB
It was not very much of an interview, because Freddie knew little or nothing about nursing or anything to do with it.

And I didn't know anything about papermaking. It was just the idea of starting a new project in the mill for the welfare of the people there. It was '58, '59, roughly that. Then I left in January '65, so I was five, six years there. I went round the mill. I think it was Freddie and the chief chemist actually took me round to see the basic workings of the mill. And smiled benignly, I suppose, and I went pottering around on my own from there when I wanted to.

They didn't have job specifications. I just created the job myself. It was fairly new. And it was a case of finding out as one went along. But what I did was, I knew a chap who worked in Thynes, the carton manufacturers.[3] He was a friend of my husband and he was the welfare and personnel officer over there, so I went over to see what their set-up was. They didn't have any nursing personnel there as such, but I went over to see what they did. And just had a general sort of nosey around. And the rest was just common sense. I had no budget given. But if I wanted something, and it was for the employees, then it was necessary and that was all.

The basic thing was to know the staff, to have a filing system, so as when they did come in it was a routine thing. I had a list of all the people within the mill, all the workers. All had various medicals when they entered it, or people who needed eye tests, people who needed to attend the doctor. I had a normal nurse's uniform, a white coat so I was easily recognisable. Basically so as they knew who I was. I used to be in at about eightish, between eight and nine. I don't think I actually officially started probably till nine o'clock, but I'd be in before that. I would go up on any medicals that were due, visit the people and go out to the schools (with a view to recruitment). Day-to-day things – going round chatting to people, seeing if the ones who had been ill how they were. Attending the safety meetings – we sometimes had to go to some lectures and stuff on safety. I took Freddie to one famous one, and I don't think I took him to any more because he collapsed when he saw some accident.

My office was in the finishing house, called the salle. Just a little room that we made up there and kitted out with files and anything I wanted. We had a couch there if it was necessary. We had the ability to have the doc when he came in to do all the various tests and stuff like that. Not very much – medical, blood pressure equipment and stuff like that. And basically just a little above first aid, because obviously if there was anything really dangerous I could just whisk them into hospital straightaway. So that there was no sort of problem with that. But basic sort of equipment and lots of pills and potions, normal sort of remedies.

And of course we had blood transfusion units visiting. They used to come out for people to give blood. And the x-ray machines for the annual x-rays, because the machines came round and they did some. Anybody who had any problems, I knew of them because they were on file. Anything that cropped up in the course of the time we just checked that they were okay, if they had to go back to hospitals and stuff. And if they were due to go into hospital for routine examinations or x-rays, or if they had to have a problem investigated. Or see the doctor or get eyes tested. Just generally day-to-day things like that, to see that everything was ticking over as it should. The daily routines – it sounded as if I didn't do an awful lot, but it was amazing, one was ticking over most of the time just seeing to their basic welfare of three or four hundred [workers].

But time was of the essence, you know. They'd go into an outpatient department and their appointment was ten o'clock, and about half past eleven they'd be taken. Whereas when I went with them I had an inroad into the staff and say, 'Look I'm sorry, this guy's losing money by being here and how could you facilitate it?' But it was just very basic. And as I say, I knew all the various medics in the area, and could go into the infirmary with any patients and cut a bit of the red tape because I knew the place. Because they lost money, and I think we lose sight of it when you are working in hospital; people are patients and they should live up to the name and sit there and wait for hours sometimes. I'll tell you a story about one of them that happened. A chap was going to the medical inspection from the army, he'd lost a leg during the war, and he had to go every year to the medical inspections board to check that his leg – well, obviously they thought his leg might grow on again. Stupid. And that's the kind of stupidity that we sort of got over by my going into it and saying to them, 'Come on, cut the rubbish, see the patient and let them get home.' And it helped both sides. Helped both that they were working, that they didn't lose money, and the speed and time in which they could get into hospital or wherever they were going and come back again. Mind you, one day it was too speedy, because I had a crash with a chap who'd had a broken arm and we demolished a wall between us. When the police arrived, because I was in my uniform they said, 'Oh, that quick putting on a plaster.' And I said, 'No, he had the plaster before!'

When I worked in the paper mill it was good because you saw where they worked, what happened to them if they had an accident in the mill and what happened to them afterwards in their home situation. I did a course in that when I went to Galloways, after I had started. To know the sort of things that one should and shouldn't do, going into people's homes and not intruding but at the same time seeing what was happening, you know.

The Doctor and Welfare Provision

And our local doctor, well, the first one when I went there, was eccentric to say the least. He was charming, but he was an individual. He would give all the youngsters who came into the mill a medical when they arrived. Just a very basic medical: their ability to see, to speak, their physique. We had one very big laddie, obese was an understatement, and the doctor would give him a bit of advice and just sort of keep an eye on him, just to see that he didn't endanger himself or anybody else with his inability – you know, just purely overeating and under-exercise. Well, we'd try to encourage them to do things like that.

The doctor, he was a delightful man, and they all thought he was slightly nuts. In the summertime he used to wear his panama hat and you knew that summer had come. And in the winter his bowler hat. He'd reverse up the village in his car because it was much easier than going up and turning at the top. He would go round and see patients of his own surgery when he was past his retiral age, the older people. Really he was supposed to do it anyhow, anybody over eighty should be visited and still is the case – meant to be visited once a month for their welfare, but it doesn't happen. But he would say to me, 'Oh, I don't think old Jock's so good, maybe have a wee nip in and see,' and we would do that. And he was an awfy nice man, but he wasn't as daft as he was painted. He'd come in and turn down their cabbage and stuff like that, but he was checking that they were actually eating properly and that they weren't boiling away all the goodness in their food.

The welfare aspect of it was quite interesting, too. I found it quite interesting, and I think that the people in the place benefited too. For instance, at Christmastime we used to go round delivering Christmas parcels to the people who'd retired. Because we knew their social circumstances. Some perhaps didn't really need much; others did. And in a subtle way you could give them stuff. Basically they got the usual cake and something to drink, perhaps these tins of ham and stuff like that, you know the very basic things. So I went round and delivered it and they were very sociable. And they'd try to encourage you, 'Oh, you'll have a wee dram?' The plants in the Balerno district flourished from whiskey tots being poured on them! But no, but that was another thing, you see, it was rather nice that they all got that. And if there was any invitations, they were all invited to go to the function at the New Year, the people that had retired. So it was a well-knit society.

Home Visits

If people were off sick I went to visit them. And also seeing sometimes if their situation at home wasn't all that hey-nonny, and perhaps improving things if we could for them. You know, the social aspect, if people had a problem with their housing. Because they had houses which were owned by the mill, and people rented it, fairly nominal rent, and depending on the seniority of the people too. Four in a block, very adequate. None of them were far from the mill, obviously. They were within, as it were, hailing distance.

The chap who was in charge of the finishing house, as they called the salle, he had a house quite close and it was a detached, very nice little property. And the chemist, he had one along the Lanark Road. But the actual mill workers themselves had quite a few of them up at Bavelaw, I think it was called. Beyond the mill, going up into Balerno itself.

And then there was a lot of the people in the local authority housing, of course, in Balerno itself. A lot of them were related and interrelated – as Freddie Ainslie said to me on one occasion, 'Don't go by people's names, just go by what they look like.'

There was one lass in particular, she was an awfully nice girl. And she had a bit of trauma in her life. I think her mother died early and she had problems generally. I remember once having to take her to Longmore Hospital and she wouldn't go in. Well, she wouldn't go to Longmore Hospital, and I couldn't understand why she didn't, so I arranged to take her, and it transpired her mother had died there. In her day, when her mother died it was what they used to know as the cancer hospital, and that was the reason. She thought that people went in and died and nobody explained to her why or whatever. And she thought that was the only type of person that went into there. Wee fears like that but get built up out of all proportion and she didn't have anybody to talk about it. She, in actual fact, probably counselled me more than I did her. Because patients you tend to find are like that. You get something extra. You couldn't explain why, you know, that at that age that she should have a malignancy like that. Somebody to talk to is important – it's not what they say. Because you don't, at the end of the day, take people's advice. Really, you are only just bouncing off your ideas. And if they don't look horrified, you realise that you're quite right.

Accident Committee
We had an accident committee just checking things that did happen. The chief engineer was on it, a Mr Gordon Russell. And Walter Smith [chief electrician]. And myself. Freddie [Ainslie] was sort of half-capacity, because blood

and he were not good friends. If he saw any, he died of fright. By and large it was a fairly safety-conscious place, because the engineer and the electrician were both very much aware of the dangers there could be, particularly in their departments. You know, things that could crop up. They would spot dangerous problems that could arise, and we tried to stop anything happening. And if anything did happen, find out why. And of course the Health and Safety people go to the factories in an instant when there's any problem. The guillotine was particularly dangerous, you know. It cut the paper and people who worked it sometimes became a bit blasé. The guard maybe should be down and they'd say, 'Och, I can do it quicker if I don't.' Of course they would have accidents. It was really carelessness, a lot of it. It was caused not by the fact that the factory was in itself negligent.

But there was one thing that startled me. We started a laddie of about sixteen, it must have been early '60s. And you know he couldn't read or write. And it was only when he came into the factory that this was discovered – how dangerous! Not the fact that he was incapable of reading and writing, but the fact that he'd gone through school and couldn't read 'No Entry' or 'Safety Beware', or whatever. He couldn't read that. In actual fact, I was staggered to find quite a lot of his generation couldn't read and write. Now that was in the '60s, terrible.

We tried to persuade him [to learn to read], but psychologically it was very difficult. Now people are much more aware of the fact that other people are incapable of reading and writing, but then there was a stigma attached to it. I mean, he had to ask what it said on a bus. He could recognise, because he had to, numbers. And this particular boy was quite clever, because he'd gone through school masking the fact that he couldn't read or write. Basically because the teacher probably heaved him to the back of the class and ignored him. But in actual fact, he'd wanted to learn but he'd just lacked encouragement, or courage to say to the teacher, 'No, I can't.' Which was sad. But you know how dangerous it is, you can't go to a factory if you can't read and write, then it's terrible.

There were sad cases in what we had. When I was there two people were actually killed in the factory. And I went out obviously to tell the next of kin what had happened. It's an awful thing if a policeman appears at your door, or you get a phone call to say something like that. So obviously that was one of things that one could do.

First Aiders

There was a first aider in both the machine shops which were at the other side of the road, the metal workers and engineers. And the actual shop floor itself. Yes, there were people who were trained first aiders. There was one that we had that was very good in the machine shop. And they had first-aid kits, but fairly basic. I think probably only two, one of them where paper was actually being made and coming onto the reels and over, and one for minor abrasions in the other place.

Galloways Buildings

Balerno was Galloways. They had what's called a machine shop, which was going up the main road on the right-hand side, where they made the heavy machinery and stuff that was needed, and repairs. The electrical people were all there. And on the other side below the main building was the lab where the chemists and everybody worked. Then the actual main building of the admin block. Then the finishing department, and beyond that was the esparto grass house and the wood pulp, and then away up at the top they had the septic tanks, I think that's what they were called. And various things that cleansed the water. Which of course had to be cleansed before it went into the Water of the Leith – that was the chemist's job, of course, to check all that.

Beyond that were the garages where they had the lorries that transported the paper south, wherever it was going. They had about three large Octopus which transported all the paper down south to the various places.[4] Because they serviced the likes of the high-quality gloss paper, *Tatler*, *Country Gardens*, that sort of paper.

Employment from Calder

Well, the village where we were in, Balerno, was quite small. And they were mostly all employed from there, but of course the workforce didn't enlarge particularly obviously. It was fairly contained. So we wanted to look further afield to see if there were other places of expertise or people who were willing to work. And where you found it a lot was in the Calder region – East, West Calders – men who'd been unemployed when shale mining and all that sort of situation closed down. And they hadn't been working for many years. Because to get from the Calder regions into town was a fairly long time, and we ran buses into the mill with the view that they would be able to get to and from their work easily.

We set it up, got a bus firm to do it on a regular basis, and we found it worked. And they were very, very good. The firm was really very good, in my opinion anyway, to the workforce. For instance, there was a glorious one – we had an old joiner who was ninety-two, Jock Pow. He used to walk over the Pentland Hills every Saturday. It was quite incredible. He decided he was going to retire, and he went to see old Mr Galloway, who himself was in his nineties. He said he was leaving, and Mr Galloway said, 'And you'll be having a pension?' And the old boy said, 'Oh no, I was too old to go on to the pension in 1936.' He was too old to get into it because he was of a particular age. You see the old boy [Mr Galloway] instituted this pension fund in the '30s, which apparently was unheard of in other industries. 'Oh,' Mr Galloway said, 'That's a terrible thing.' So he gave him a wee pension. You know that sort of give and take with the employer and employed, which was good.

Individual Financial Problems

I think they had a sliding scale of being paid a certain amount from the mill when they were off. Because obviously they got something from the government as well when they were off sick. So they would get that. But if they were really stuck for – maybe they were starting to owe money here there and everywhere – the firm would be informed that they were not able to meet their commitments, and why. And then of course their wages were, the word escapes me, I think sequestered might have been it. Anyway it was taken at source so that their wives would be able to pick up the money rather than the men. Because sometimes some of them picked up their wages on a Friday, went down to the bookie shop and went home with little or nothing.

But there again, one knew the problems. The women – to begin, they weren't very keen to sort of say, obviously, anything about it. But they did eventually say, you know, well they had problems and they couldn't buy this, that or the next thing because their wages had gone. But there weren't many like that – one or two, and it could create problems, of course.

Women Workers

I interviewed some of them, the girls in particular, to see if they were suitable for working in the salle. Because in essence it was a very boring job, the finishing department where the girls principally worked. You had to know that they knew what they were doing, that they wouldn't be bored. We found initially that if girls came from town that had been offered a job, they didn't last long. So we thought we would perhaps be better to try and root out the ones that we didn't think would last the pace. So I had a say in that, but just as people, not as papermakers or finishers or whatever. That was left up to the manageress in the finishing department, or clerical staff. Mr Ainslie himself would do it, or whichever department they were going to go to.

I saw them after they were actually employed and had an interview with them, and then sent them on for their medical. And the doctor would come up whenever we needed him to take two or three people at a time, say, to do a medical on them when they arrived. It was just to check for ourselves that they were fit and able, because if anything happened in the interim we would know why.

The woman who did the work in the finishing house never ceased to amaze me. Unlike men working on a production line, I mean these women could be sitting there and they'd be doing the paper finishing and they'd be chatting away about where they'd been last night and where they were going tomorrow. And they would be noticing every minute that anything was wrong with the paper when it came out. But they didn't appear to be doing it now. We tried doing it with some men, and we sent them up to the finishing house and they stopped because they couldn't speak and do it at the same time. Whereas the women would be chattering away nonstop, and you'd think – they can't possibly be doing it – but they were, they were doing an incredible amount of work.

They had the forelady, I think she was called, in the finishing house, and she showed them the rudiments of the work. They adapted very quickly, because a lot of them had always come from papermaking families. Here you would get the generations coming through, so they knew all about it and were very adept at it. And as I say, they could do it effortlessly. Talk about Jeannie and Johnny and how this had happened and everything, and it was quite incredible. There were no repetitive injuries in these days. Nobody ever said, 'Oh, it's because I've been [constantly doing the same action].' No, I don't know, it's amazing the new maladies that have come in to working practice. It never dawned on us, eight hours a day and it was the same action, it must have been on their wrists all the time. But yeah, I think probably their natural breaks solved it.

CANTEEN

Mrs Anderson ran the canteen. Basically, it had all the meals; actually it was pretty good quality stuff. We went up every so often to check it was running smoothly and hygiene top notch. When they had what they called a shutdown, I used to run the canteen. Not the cooking of it, just the taking of the money and to see everything was hot. Because obviously there were very few staff there. There were people who were on the maintenance staff there, and it was much easier that they still had food and things to have, because they were working all the time. So a skeleton staff would have been on doing the actual cooking, and I was just serving and helping generally.

They had hot meals always. They would have to have them – they would have gone on strike without having a hot meal! Very basic, mince and potatoes and stews and stuff like that. And Mrs Anderson used to run it with a rod of iron. Aye, she was really quite funny. She used to get quite annoyed if they questioned the fact that it wasn't very good. It was always pretty clean and well-organised, and she had her people who did all the work, you know. She had three helpers and herself. The canteen was on the first floor, because obviously it was much more central with all the parts of the firm coming together.

They had two sittings. And they didn't necessarily all come in at once – 12.30, then 1 o'clock, they would stagger it. Well, it was automatically staggered, because if you were working on the machine shop, for instance, making the actual paper – probably say there were six of them working there – two or three would go off at a time. And so they would work it that way. And the lab would come in at a different time. And the various other people, the drivers, and it was a rota basis. But not strict – a rolling sort of situation. And it would probably run from about twelve to half past one actually serving the meals. And they could go for specified breaks, an afternoon cup of tea. No, it was really pretty organised.

Making Paper

It was fascinating to see the paper being made. I mean, [before joining Galloways], I had patients coming in, and if they said they worked in a papermill, I would think, 'Oh, yeah.' I'd not a clue what they were actually talking about, so it was quite nice to see it, quite revealing to see how people worked in their various industries. The first time I saw it being made from this grass and wood pulp and all this watery stuff, and suddenly you get paper at the end of it. Quite fascinating.

Esparto grass, the ingredient for papermaking, was imported from Algeria when we got it. That was at the time when they had – I can never remember the name of the terrorists, not terrorists, but they were freedom fighters allegedly in Algeria at the time, you know, trying to free Algeria from France. And at one point, I think it might have been one of the mills down in Penicuik way, in a consignment of esparto grass they found a hand grenade, and they got the bomb squad in!

Factory Fire Brigade
I never actually saw it, but I believe they had their own fire brigade at one point. But it sadly deteriorated, because the helmets were utilised, now what were they for? Plants? Axes were obviously used in people's back gardens – the various bits of equipment sort of vanished overnight. But they had a small fire engine in the days before a proper fire brigade was in vogue. Because I think they'd been papermaking on that site for a long time before Galloways went into it. I'm not sure they volunteered, but then towards the time when I was there, that had gone. But they still had supposedly the ability to put out a fire, although I would have doubted it very much.

Mill Noise
The mill itself was noisy. I mean, you couldn't really carry on a conversation in the part where they were actually rolling the machinery down – the thing vibrated, as it were.

So the noise was really quite colossal. It was not excessively noisy in so much as they didn't have to wear earpieces or anything to stop that. You didn't find that people suffered from, say, tinnitus or anything like that because of the excessive noise. Nor did they become deaf at a particular stage. I think it was the kind of factory that actually, although it was noisy, was not excessively noisy, as in some industries obviously that are drilling or heavy heat and stuff like that. There was nothing excessive.

Social Functions
It was a close-knit community. They had a function every year – everybody went from all sort of positions in the mill. A dance was held in what was called the Charlotte Rooms in these days, you know Charlotte Street in Edinburgh, a large function room up there. And they had a dinner dance, and it was attended by any and everybody who felt so inclined, usually about January. And it was a very social occasion. But also recreational facilities, because they had tennis courts at Galloways, and the staff could play there – it was very much a community built round the mill. They had a bowling green, football pitches and we also helped to organise the annual Currie and Balerno gala. They all got retirement functions, but again they kept them within their own department. You know, if it was somebody from the electrical workshop they would have a little retiral thing, but they didn't have any retiral gifts or anything for people. They would see Mr Galloway when he was still alive – that was why the old joiner went to see him when he was retiring, he was asked about his pension, so they obviously went to see him on their retiral, a nicety not enjoyed by today's workforce.

MANAGEMENT

But it was that kind of firm; old Mr Galloway himself was good that way. Well, as he went on working himself until his mid-nineties, he was well aware of continuity. Old John, he was a nice old man. He'd come in most days. When I saw him, well, he'd be in his late eighties when I first met him. And he pottered in at about eleven o'clock, or maybe nearer twelve. And his driver would take him home, and then he would come in maybe in the afternoon for the odd hour or so. He took a keen interest, the old boy, and I think he knew everything that was going on, although I don't know that aspect of it. The old sort of fashioned employer you don't see nowadays.

And his nephew, Jack Haig, took over from him. When Mr Haig took over, nothing much changed. Really, it was probably run by the administrator; in other words, Freddie Ainslie probably did most of it. Then they did take on a general manager, a chap called Walton, and then it became a bit less personal after that. I wasn't there long after that. I don't think he was of the same inclination as old Mr Galloway had been originally. You had to be, I suppose, more commercially minded. I remember we were going round investigating other outfits other than the high-powered paper, if there was a possibility of making tissue and stuff like that. We were going round investigating all the various tissues: toilet and facial tissues and things like that. Just to see if there was a possibility of an offshoot. Because I think by that time probably the high-class paper was starting to be imported cheaper than it could be produced in Britain. Certainly things started to go down at that point.

When I left, '64, '65, things were starting not to be terribly apparent, but it was different with a general manager in charge or whatever he was called, managing director I think was his title; it was just different. It wasn't a family any longer, you know; it wasn't a family-run firm. So I think there was a much greater degree of commercialism in it. The workforce probably felt that it wasn't quite such a friendly atmosphere. And then it started to go down, as all papermills did, and then finally Galloways was sold off and the land was developed as the village grew and grew.

Notes
1. Company secretary at John Galloway & Sons.
2. The industrial nurse provided in-house assistance in the event of an accident.
3. William Thyne, Lochend Works, Marionville Road [Lithography and Letterpress Printing].
4. John Galloway had three Octopus lorries.

Nan Aitken

I WENT for an interview for a job at fourteen from school. My sister worked there, and my brother before he went to the airforce. We stayed here and my mother couldn't afford us to travel to the town, and it was all there was in the district, so that was how I landed there. I started down the pits, bagging the shavings, as the saying goes, bagging the shavings. Do you know what I started with? Ninety-nine pence. That was my weekly wage, for a year, and it went up a shilling.

I did that for a full two year, maybe more. One or two older ones that came in went in to learn the overhauling; they didn't go on the machines. It was just the younger ones that were on the machines. We worked half past six in the morning and we stopped for half an hour at breakfast, then we stopped for an hour at dinner. I used to have to run all the road down and all the road back. It was an hour generally, but it takes you ten minutes to a quarter of an hour to run all the road and the same back, you know to see to my mother, because she wasnae able to do things, you see. And that was it at five o'clock. Then the time's changed and it was half past seven, then latterly it was eight o'clock. When you were older the times all changed for everybody.

NAN AITKEN

WORKING THE MACHINES

It was a messy job at the beginning when you were on the [cutter] machines – you still got fluff off the paper, you know, when it moved – but not dirty like when you were on the machines. When you were on machines, it was very dirty. Up the stair where they made the paper, after it had come from the one boiler up to the other boiler, when they put all the bleach and stuff in it, it was horrible the smell, you know. Then I went on to the cutter, just making sure that the paper kept flowing onto the pallets. Generally each machineman had their own workers. There was one down the pit, and one at the paper when it came in, when it was cut, and the man that worked the machine.

OVERHAULING AND COUNTING

You see, you went right through to the other place, from the cutter house where I worked first, you went right through to the back end, and then worked your ways up to the salle. At the other end of the building, they took the paper. They kept a lot of paper that wasnae so good for us to train on, and then we learnt to overhaul on older paper. Then they brought good paper for us and you learnt, you kept the bad from the good. Course, the bad went back up the mill to be remade. But eventually your work was going as good, although you were still down at the end your paper was going through. From there, at the bottom you came into the main salle, and that was when you were on your own.

The paper that you had to look at, you got it given to you as a bundle, very heavy. Because when they dished the paper out to you, it was on pallets. Two men worked the pallets, and they used to measure off a bundle, say that much, and phoned it over and you had to lift it. They helped you, you know, but it was very heavy. Then you walked from the floor to your own stance with this paper to overhaul it, and we got corner things to fit the paper into. And you drew it over like that, all the way across. Each sheet, each sheet went over until you had quite a bundle – and then you lifted it and put it on a back table. And that's where it was counted from. Someone else counted it from there, and then the tiers tied it from there – they lifted each ream, it was in reams – and they tied it on their tables.

After many years, many years, I got on the finishing – well, the finishing was the counting. It was much easier. I hadn't so much lifting to do, and I was a good bit older.

You had two rubbers on your finger – just pieces of rubber, they used to cut it off for you – and you put it on to draw the paper. And you drew them, well it was all day hurting your fingers in there. And your fingers were so sore, because you had to learn to fan it and four at a time. And then so many quires to a ream. Twenty-four in a quire, when you did ten quire, you made a ream. There was two elderly ladies, sisters, used to go up and down, and they used to fan up some of the paper to see if the work was getting done properly. Otherwise there was nobody touched anybody else's work. We had our own office so that's where there was a boss and a girl and a man in the office. They worked in conjunction with the main office.

The cutters made a terrible noise, but down in the salle it wasnae noisy, it was quiet. But the machine house it was – really the cutters were going all the time, you see, where there was one, two, three, four cutters and a winder that they were going all day, so there was plenty noise.

Holidays
Well, we never got any holidays; we never even got Christmas Day when I started to work. New Year's Day

was the only day you got off, until many years after – you could take a holiday but you got no wages. No work, no pay. Then, oh I don't know when it was they started, that you got your one week's holiday, but you always got Christmas and New Year after that. Christmas Day and New Year's Day. Kinleith, at the beginning they didn't – but they did for a while after that – close for trades week. But it was just one week. Some people took a fortnight, took their week that was stated plus an extra week. But then that was at their own expense, and there's not very many could afford that.

WAGES

There was a wages guy. You got paid on a Thursday and it was at the office where you go in, when you went in to the mill. You went in and you clocked in, and went out a door and then into the factory. Well, there was a window there, and the pay clerk came and paid you your wages from that window, on a Thursday. Your wee tin box and your money was in it. He just gave you a number and he handed you the box, and there was a wee slot at the side and you put the box down the slot, and that was you.

STRIKE

They went on strike at our place one day, but it was just a farce of a strike. I don't remember what they wanted – it was just the women, though, it wasn't the men. It only lasted half a day, or a day or something. I remember this as plain as anything, because I'll tell you why, the foreman came up the floor and as he passed me he says, 'I'm surprised at you striking, Nan.' And I didn't strike; I couldnae afford to strike; I didn't strike, but he said that. But, you see, once they were all out, you had just to stand still, you couldn't do anything, they wouldnae help you till they sorted it out.

Union Holiday Homes

We were in the unions. I think eventually you automatically went into it. But everybody in other places didn't go – some were mixed about, you know – but we were in the papermakers' union. We didn't pay individually; it was kept off at wages. They sorted all that. I never, ever went to a union meeting, but they had meetings every so often. See, they were away down in Leith; the union office was down in Leith.

And they had union holiday homes, supposed to be for people who had been sick, you know? I been on holiday with the union, oh many years ago. It was a beautiful place. One in Brighton and one in Ayr, but I never went to the one in Ayr. But I know some people that did. I know a chap that used to go every year to Ayr; he never kept well and he used to go for his holidays every year to the home at Ayr. Two or three of the residents made the supper, for it was just biscuits and tea, and it was left to the residents to make it for anybody that wanted it. But all the rest of the meals were made for you. They had an office in the town and you had to go and apply, then it went through the channels, to see if you were eligible to go. We had to have a doctor's line of course, to go – medical grounds – and they gave us our fare and pocket money. It wasn't very much, but it was enough to do you, I think a fortnight, that's the longest you get, a fortnight.

Transport

Long ago, it was just local people. Between Balerno and Juniper Green, no further. See Balerno had a papermill, as you know. A lot of people worked in Balerno papermill, but a lot of people worked from Balerno, Currie and Juniper Green in Kinleith Mill. But when they stopped getting workers, they opened up and they were coming from the town to work in the paper mills. They came on the bus. The railway ran through Kinleith right to Balerno, that was the end of it. The train turned there, and then came back to go back to Edinburgh. Then of course the goods train came up, and it went into the siding at the mill to get loaded, if they were using the train. The esparto grass came in lorries. And pulp, woodpulp came in lorries and went down the hill to the mill in lorries. There was quite a bit of stuff came in the train, but the lorries were the main thing. They had their own lorry for doing odd jobs, and they had their own full-time drivers.

MILL ACCIDENTS

There was a man killed one time in the mill. He was drawn into the machine, but he must've gone too near, must've touched the rollers and they drew him in. That's only one that I knew that anything serious happened to. But there would be lots of wee bits of accidents. There was supposed to be guards on lots of machines but a lot of the men used to take them off, because it was a nuisance for them, you know. Used to pick them up, you know, a guard if it was like on a machine, and they would pick it up. Of course, they had to do that to sort it when it got mixed up. But then some of them never put them back down again. Dangerous. It was risky, very risky. Your hair could get caught, anything, on the machines.

WARTIME

Oh, we entered short time quite a few times. We termed it short time if there was no work. And we'd maybe work three days on and three days off. One week on and one week off. Because they had no orders, you know. Towards the end of the war was just bad times. I was warden in the street I used to stay, they didn't call me up. I was at home with my mother, but I volunteered to do ammunition work but I was never called up which was good for my mother.

Annual Outings

Going back many, many years ago they used to have a trip, as we called it a trip, once a year. I don't know how long maybe – I can only remember about three times I was ever there, but the firm laid it on. They laid it on because you had to have a train or coaches or something to take you. One time we went to Rothesay, I remember that. I can't remember where the other places we went – three or four times we were away, but just once a year, though. I think the married ones were allowed to take their wives. But I mean, I was just on my own, with the rest of the girls that were working, you know. I don't think they let outsiders go, but a husband could take his wife.

But there was nothing here for entertainment, nothing like that; you had to make your own entertainment. There was a dance hall in Currie. There wasnae a dance hall in Juniper, but there was a dance hall in Colinton, but really nothing in Juniper for anybody, you know. Kids had their clubs, but not for working folk. Well, there was a village hall up there; they used to have like a wee guild or something like that in the village hall, but for anything else, nothing. I'm afraid I wasn't a modern dancer, I went in for old-time dancing, but I had to go to the town for that.

NAN AITKEN

Mill Houses
In Blinkbonny, the mill built for the employees a big block of houses, and a lot of the people that stayed in Juniper Green moved up to Blinkbonny Mill property. That belonged to the mill, and there was a block down Belmont Avenue belonged to the mill. They had quite nice houses at Blinkbonny, of course, when they built them. The rents were just average, you know, what everybody else was paying. There was two houses at Blinkbonny at the side of the big flats where the head engineer and the joiner and them stayed.

Mr Bruce
Mr Bruce, I knew him quite well, his wife too, and his son. They used to stay down the road there. He used to walk up the railway, because he knew times of the trains, you see, and into the mill through the railway. And he would go up to his office – he had a posh office – and he would get all the news of what had been going on throughout the day, or if he was away anywhere he got all the news. Then him and the underforeman used to walk right round the mill. They didn't stop; they just walked round taking note of everything as they were going round. And every day while he was here, if he was away, well the other man did it himself, just to see that everything was going right. Mr Bruce was a nice person, very nice person.

Closing the Mill
I was fifty-one when it closed. It came as a very big shock to everybody, a very big shock to everybody. You see, when we did get told, you wouldn't dare leave because if you left you wouldn't have got your bonus or whatever you call it – redundancy. If you had left between them telling you and

the date of them closing, you got nothing. But if you stayed on you got it. Hundred and eighty pound. So what could you do with that? I mean it was what you were allowed. I mean now they get thousands of pounds when they're redundant, but not in these days; it was a hundred and eighty pound.

John Tweedie, the foreman, he tried lots of firms to try and get work for as many as he could, you know. And well, I don't know where any papermills, other than Balerno, if anybody went to Balerno, that would be the only place, because nobody else had any qualifications for anywhere else. And these other people packed in, you know. Course, some of the older men retired, because, see, you could work till you were ninety in the papermill. Nobody said boo to you, as long as you were able to work.

Well, he tried several places, and it was those and such as those that got the jobs, if you understand. But by that time I was staying in Smithfield Street in Gorgie. And there was a gentleman stayed in the foot of my stair where I stayed, and he got to hear that I was gonna be made redundant, and he called me into his house one night. And he says, 'I've heard that you're losing your job, Nan', but he says, 'I'll give you a wee tip, you go up to Waddies in Slateford Road and ask to see a Mr Dickson, and see what he says to you.' So I duly did of course, but this was before the mill shut and I went up to see him, and I explained that the mill was shutting. He says, 'Is there more people?' and I said, 'Oh yes, there's quite a few looking for work.' So he says to me, 'Well, I could maybe take on about five of you throughout our factory' – that was the printing trade – 'see how you get on.'

1. Mill buildings at Kinleith Mill showing large mill chimney nicknamed Willies Lum

2. Office buildings at John Galloway & Sons' Balerno Bank Mill

3. The last special on the Balerno branch line passes Inglis Mill, 19th April 1965

4. Machine house at Kinleith Mill

5. Women working overhauling paper in the salle at Kinleith Mill

6. The lab at Kinleith Mill

7. Woodhall Thistle football team in 1931

8. A Christmas dance at Galloways of Balerno

'Mary Reid'

MY grandfather, my father, my uncle, my aunts, most of them were all there. My father worked in the turbine house. My uncle, he worked in the cutterhouse, where they cut the paper on the winders before they went on webs. And my grandfather, he worked with what they called the pug.[1] When the trains, the good trains, came in for the paper, there was a siding. He had this sort of thing that pulled the carriages into the mill for the paper and different things that were brought in. My grandfather just pottered around. He had his wee weighing machine, and the weighing machine for the lorries coming in and going out. And that was right at his office.

I started in 1937 in July. I was fourteen. The gaffer lived two or three doors away. He asked if there was [anyone available to fill] vacancies because 'we're needing workers'. He heard that I had been leaving school, so he said, 'Oh, just tell her start on Monday.' I left school on the Friday and started on the Monday. But I was going to Guide camp, so I got my holidays three weeks later – that was a condition. And that was it. It was only about three doors away, so we all knew each other. So I didn't get much choice.

I started through the cutter house for two, three years. Very menial jobs of catching the shavings coming off the machines round it. And putting it into sacks. We had to go down pits. Not I – some of them had deeper pits than I ever had – I had a good cutter man. I was a wee bit inquisitive, and as the young men were going away to war I helped big Jim on almost everything on the cutter, even to loading it. But I wasn't supposed to. I liked working with the machinery. We were sometimes sent down to different departments if we were quiet, and again we helped. And I helped two old men with the paper, tying the paper and throwing it up.

Overhauling

And then I went through and learnt the overhauling. We started at half past six in the morning until about half past five at night. But we got an hour for our breakfast and then we got an hour for our lunch. We only did that for about a year and then it was changed until we began at half past seven. But they did away with the breakfast time, and we got our ten minutes' break, and then we still had our lunchtime – Monday to Saturday. At the latter end we worked until half past ten on a Saturday morning. We could work until twelve, but after half past ten, for the next hour and a half it was overtime.

In the wintertime, sometimes the snow was as high as the hedges, and we'd all sort of meet and help each other down to the mill. My mother would make up sandwiches. Then there was pipes – it wasn't radiators and things – it was pipes that ran underneath, and we used to lay our sandwiches on the pipes to heat them. There was a hotplate for getting the boiling water. The men would get the hotplate and they could lay it on the hot pipe and that's where they made the tea. So, we had our good times.

There was an old lady with her skirts, you know, right old-

'MARY REID'

fashioned with her white pinny, her white overall thing in front of her, always this white pinny and very strict. She trained you to do the job properly before you got on to do actual overhauling. She would sometimes come along and just look through your work to see if there was anything that shouldn't be there. Oh, they were strict then. As far as I remember there was two sisters and another lady. We always called her Highland Mary and the two sisters. And they did check on the work.

You overhauled it, someone came and counted it in reams, and once it was put into reams the men – tiers – came and they tied it and put it in the wrapping papers, etc. Then it was taken down to the baling shed, and from there it was taken up to the gangway where the wagons came in. And that was taken away by two lorry drivers. They took a lot. But I presume they did local trips.

WAGES

I must have been one of the first rebels. Once I was doing the men's work, and they got paid more than we did.[2] And I said, if I ever do their work I wanted their wages. In the end I got it. It was only five shillings. Which is what, about twenty-five pence or something? But it was a lot of money then. Our wages were eleven shillings and sevenpence halfpenny. I always remember that halfpenny. And that was our weekly wage.

We worked on piecework, and there was someone dividing it out. You all got the same measurements and they always sent a line round every week. And the top overhauler, the wage was put on and then you judged. In other words, the more [bad paper] you took out, the less pay you got. Which caused another little rebellion. Because we said that because we were trying to do it thoroughly we were being victimised for it. If we'd been a bit careless, you know, we'd have got more money.

Sometimes you got half days if there wasn't enough work to do. That didn't happen a great deal. I think there was once – I was still a junior then, and I don't really remember the story – but we were put off work and we went to sign on the dole. And they got the princely sum of three shillings and ninepence.

In '55 I went back for a few weeks to train again, you know, just for a few weeks to get back into my stride. And then to fill in for anyone off. And then eventually we got our own stance. It was just one long bench, but you each had your own box at your side that you could use to sit on and keep your coat and your belongings in and that. And the pipes run underneath so you got your heat from the boiler. Sometimes, if the heat was on it was awful.

Overhauling Different Paper

The Bible paper, it was very thin and it was large, and there was a lot who couldn't do [overhaul] it. If you could get the knack of it, then it was alright. And in fact, sometimes we were put into twos to do it – luckily, I was one of them that could get the knack of it – when you pulled it away, sort of give it a flick.

And we made certain paper that was really top, good quality. Balerno Mill, they made a different type of paper. They made it for banknotes and things like that. They were different altogether from us. And we made a lot of paper for Blackie's books and children's annuals.[3] The Bible paper, it only came in periodically, obviously. Of which we were glad. And then you got something else – it was an angle. Big angle, it was cut at an angle and had like a double glazing on it.

'MARY REID'

Some of it even went abroad, as far as I know. Because I remember down at what they called the baling shed, they put the labels and that on. Then it was put into a press, cased in hessian and sealed, and then it was all sewed up. It was stencilled as to where it was going and I think these went abroad – that's why they were all so carefully packed.

And then sometimes we had to pull out shades, dress them up and put them in separate. And occasionally there was someone who had put a roll of paper in upside down so the cut was different, so you had to turn it. Some of them just pulled it out, but if it was reasonable some of us turned it. I think it was because we had the training that the latter ones didn't have, and we could turn it and just go along without having all this palaver of pulling it to the side. Well, they only got about six weeks' training at the latter end, whereas we had much longer than that.

GREENHOUSE

At the back of where we worked there was a greenhouse, and the gardener, he attended to these. You see it was surplus steam that kept it going. And oh, the vines, you could see the big vines through the glass. But they were used for the family. The Bruces would probably use what they wanted, but a great deal of it went to the hospitals. Oh yes, there were some peaches as well, but it was mostly grapes. We had to watch them growing them, peering through the glass. Also, at the back of the papermill, there used to be a curling pond. And that's where, in the clubhouse, the Guides held their meeting, and when we went out to play games we went down into what used to be the curling pond.

Working Conditions

That was one thing that I hated when we worked in the salle – the windows faced the north and the others south. When the sun was on the south side, it was so warm you were exhausted with the heat. But if you were moved to the other side it was fresher, and even though the windows were open these poor women had the sun beating through the glass on them. It was horrible.

And I think I must have been a wee bit of a rebel at times, because I used to get on about this heat, you see, and in the end I got shifted to the other side. I just couldn't stand the heat, never could. And he [Mr Napier] came in one day and said, 'It's amazing, it's amazing.' I said, 'What's amazing?' He says, 'You're quite cool and calm.' And he says, 'And these poor women.' I says, 'That's what I've been trying to tell you for long enough, that's what they've got to put up with. You wouldn't listen to me,' I says, 'Now you've seen it for yourself that I'm quite alright at this side, but that side and these poor women.' So they came and they covered up, sort of smoked the glass, you know? To try to keep the sun's rays off them. So it was hard work trying to work in the heat. Oh, we had a good laugh, singing away. We had some good laughs. The women were nice. I wouldn't say it was all hard work and no play. I mean, sometimes daft things happened and you just stood and laughed. We did things together and we helped each other. If you were finished your work you'd go and help somebody else. I mean we all helped each other.

We got on fairly well, and we used to go out at night. Someone would get tickets for the dances at the school in Juniper Green at the school socials, and a crowd of us would go. If we were close to our finish or our lunch hour, we'd set our hair, grips impressing in the waves. And when we had time, we used to sit and sing all the latest songs; to this day we have a friendship that goes beyond workmates.

Work Clothing

We wore our overalls. But we had a firm felt, thick to give us support to protect our fronts, and we tied this round us. It helped you when you were lifting the paper as well, gave you the support. It used to wear with the paper cutting into you, so you had to get a new one often.

The thing we had was Baird's shoes; it was a good quality shop. They used to run, was it twenty weeks? You paid so much, your number would come out the hat whatever week you were, and we would get shoes. I mean, it was one way of getting good shoes without hurting your purse.

We had a very unhygienic way of covering fingers up. You know the brown tape? Sticky tape? You could strip the gum part off it – off the back – and roll it up, and we just put that round it. That's what we used to use. We were never ill from it. The same when the women were thirsty. We would sometimes make a paper cap – when we were juniors, like – and we'd make a paper cap, go and get the fresh water, go around them all with this paper cap, and let them get their portion of water.

First Aid

I had started first aid when I was fourteen. And just latterly I was always wanting into nursing. So when the war came, they needed a first-aid team in the work. If we were ones who had trained for first aid we were part of the team. Not that we were really ever called on – cuts, someone cut their hands on glasses, or things like that, maybe. We went to the meetings and we got the princely sum of two shillings (ten pence now). It was voluntary and they had about twenty of us, mainly women, you know. And a doctor came, and a nurse, or a lecturer in first aid.

Well, we had a first-aid room built. And it was a retired police officer that was in charge of it. He was a sort of welfare, he was, and he helped. He would more or less run the first-aid classes as well. And that's where we used to hold our first-aid meetings. When we had the first-aid team there was this doctor. At the time there was Cold War sort of threats. And he wanted us to make up a sort of civil defence first-aid unit. Because he thought we were quite capable of doing it, but we weren't so keen. We were quite happy doing what we did, but he wanted to get us involved in this other community work, you know. And that's when they were building bunkers and things. Everybody was going to get there in four minutes, I don't know. I don't know what they were expecting, but they're only getting rid of some of these bunkers now that they built.

Major Accidents

There was one. I was home here, had come for my lunch and I didn't know how bad it was, and his wife lived across the road. It was one of these huge silo things, you know, and he'd fallen into it. He was an electrician. But luckily there was sludge still in the bottom, which broke his fall. But he had a bad back and was off a long, long time. But when I came home we didn't know how serious it was, or if he was still alive. I went and told my neighbour, and I says – being staff, I can't say anything; I don't want to get her alarmed – 'We don't know, someone will probably call.' And I says, 'Be on hand to be ready for her.' So my neighbour was there and then Mr – oh, I forget his name now, but he came up in the car and said that he was in hospital. But he was very ill for a long time.

'MARY REID'

WORKER REPRESENTATION

In the latter years there was sort of workers' representatives, you know. People voted for us to go in and represent them for different things, and there was a meeting held every month. This was just a year or two before the mill closed. We used to hold meetings discussing any complaints or anything.

Well, there was two or three of us chosen, and we don't know who voted for us, but you know, people voted. I can't remember how many there were, but we used to go up to the boardroom in the office with the works' manager, Ian Napier, and the likes of that. And we held meetings every month. To this day I never found out who put my name down. It was separate, had nothing to do with the union. We weren't one hundred per cent union then. I joined the union. I wouldn't say I was hundred per cent unionist, but they fought to get us rises and it was only fair you supported.

Once they were put out on strike because of the printers' strikes.[4] They were put on the dole for that, but they didn't actually go on strike, if you know what I mean. When the printers went on strike they didn't need the papers, so the papermakers had to go on the dole because of it. Well, at that particular time – I don't remember how long, because I had had a major operation and they were on strike – the doctor said to me, 'Well, after it you can start, you can start after July.' And I says, 'That means I'll have to go in and sign on again.' And the sickness benefit was the same as the dole money, and he says, 'Well, it's pointless changing; we may as well keep you on the sickness.' So I stayed on that until – I think it was about five or six weeks.

The other time, some of them walked out, they wouldnae come back. The heating had broken down, and they were so cold. It was the women that did it – I don't think the other departments did – but they were so cold that they walked out and refused to come back until there was heating. And that's the only time I remember [going on strike]. Well, they got the heating going again!

Mr Bruce

He didn't come round a lot, but you did see him sometimes. You'd see him walking through maybe to the other departments. And I believe there was other members of the family before him. He lived down at Lorimer House, down at the crossroads – it's a nursing home now.

But the main family lived up at Ravelrig. I used to go up there when I was a child and watch the hunt leaving from there every New Year's Day. It was all the colour, and I thought it was great until one day I saw the fox, and saw the hounds catching the fox just in front of our houses, and I wasn't so keen after that. But when you're young, you saw the colour and that was it.

During the War

Some of them worked on till they were a good age. There was one man and he was there till he was nearly eighty. And there was a woman – two women well into their seventies. They couldn't do the full amount of work, but they pottered on. When the war was on, I went walking up the Mill Brae with this old man, and I'm sure he was nearer eighty than seventy. I think it was a Saturday. There was three planes, and they were German planes, came right over – they must have been taking photos. And they were so low that we could see the signs right above us. No sirens or anything had gone. And there's three planes flew by. And him, old as he was at the time, with his glasses he could still see the signs on the plane. By that time, part of the factory was used for storing tea and sugar that belonged to the ministry of defence. It was all under lock and key, mind. They built air-raid shelters. At the beginning of the war, that's where we used to have our first-aid classes, before they built the first-aid room. I can't remember using it except for first-aid lectures and that.

CROWNING OF THE QUEEN

There was the parade on the Saturday or whatever day, and the Crowning of the Queen. It was Balerno that had the Crowning of the Queen. The Balerno Mill was the provider, I think. And that was held at the school, because my mother used to take us up, but we didn't get involved because we didn't belong to Balerno school. So my mother made up sandwiches, but the ones that went to Balerno school got their bags, you know. Yes. That was Galloways, but we went up and saw it. The Crowning of the Queen was usually the top of the class. Yes. It was lovely going up watching that. We didn't have anything down here like that. I would say there was more unity in Balerno than there was ever down here. They did more together, and to this day there are still certain elements that still do things together. I don't know if we either lost it or never had it.

DECLINE AND CLOSURE OF THE MILL

Oh yeah, there was a decline. One or two of us complained about how much broke we had, and he turned round and said to us, 'You were brought up in a different school,' he says. 'When you were brought up it was quality before quantity,' he says. 'I'm afraid things have changed a little and you've got to shut your eyes to some things, and it's more quantity before quality.' And then I heard a rumour from London – someone that had worked in London had a relative there – and they had said that there was a rumour that our mill would be closed the following year. And I brought this up at one of our meetings and I was more or less put down for saying it. But it did happen. It was proved that they knew in London about a year before we closed. But, oh, I put my foot in it there, I think. And it was true, we did.

And it did hit us. Oh yes, we were shocked. I mean, you'd heard rumours, but it's one thing hearing a rumour and another thing it happening. You never thought it would happen. And it was a big blow at the time. Something that came rattling out of my head in verse, and it was just this women says, 'Oh, that's good', and she started writing it down. There was a lot more, but she couldn't keep up. It's sort of the way we felt:

> A hundred and fifty year ago,
> The paper trade began to grow.
> In this lovely Currie valley,
> Beside the burn bathed deep and shally
> The burn in which the bairns wade.
> Nearby the women picking shade,
> Close east deckles, or a crest.
> At least they tried their best.
> They wandered here for many a mile,
> And sometimes thought it's not worthwhile.
> Then came the news 'twas most repugnant:
> I'm sorry, folks, but you're redundant.
> For many years in this green valley,
> We've worked, argued and been pally
> And now with hearts like lumps of lead,

'MARY REID'

> We see our valley just drop dead.
> John to share out paper tries,
> While women stand and wipe their eyes.
> And men they pace both to and fro,
> To think the papermills should go.
> The ghosts they come from out the past,
> From ominous lad to simple lass,
> To see us look for pastures new,
> And say, 'Farewell, goodbye to you.'

Someone took it up to the office, and they did quite a few copies of that. And the day we left some of us, just in our department, we got together, put two or three shillings each and bought something. And some of us made tea and some cakes and we had a cheerio and a wee song and that. Well, drink was never allowed in the factory anyway, but we all had a wee cheerio before we left amongst ourselves.

Finding a New Job

They sent people out, and word came out. The union took a hand to try and find us jobs. Waddies were wanting five people, and Susie – she was the sort of supervisor in our department – she chose five of us. Of course, they took her – she was there, and another four of us, and we went to Waddies. Well, we went for interview; we got the job. It wasn't the same; I'm not saying we didn't get on or anything, but I always said it was never the same. But some went to Balerno Mill, some went down to Thynes, and others went different roads. I think the atmosphere by then at latter days, it was beginning to change. There was a different element coming in, and they were coming in from further afield.

PAPERMAKING ON THE WATER OF LEITH

NOTES

1. Goods trains had been coming into the Kinleith siding since 1874. In 1902 Kinleith bought an electric shunter engine, which was still in use when the mill closed in 1966.
2. During the Second World War, 'Mrs Reid' undertook work roles in the mill that had been traditionally undertaken by men.
3. Kinleith Mill was the first mill to produce a bulk-basis featherweight paper. This became popular for children's books, as its use made them light and easy to carry.
4. The printing industry was out on strike during the summer of 1959.

Thallon Veitch

Now when I left school, I waited to get into the mill. And I had a good chance because my dad had worked in the mill, he'd worked with Galloway in Portobello. I was coming up for sixteen. Everybody wanted to go to the mill, maybe it took a wee while to get you in, and you done something of that, just labouring about until you got in.

Everybody wanted a job in the mill, and I eventually got one. You had to put your name down, and of course as soon as a position become available, with you having a parent there, that was a bonus. And I was lucky because when Galloways moved out to Balerno, my dad worked there for a while. But we lived a way down in the far side, west side, of Edinburgh, so travelling out here was too much and he packed up. And then he worked for Brown Brothers in Edinburgh. Mr Galloway was going round, and he said to the engineer, 'Where's Veitch?' And he says, 'Oh, he's left.' 'Look, we're building houses, and the first available house, give it to Veitch and get him back', so he must've thought something and I suppose that was a good start for me.

My dad was a turner brass finisher, and he worked seven days a week. When I was twenty-one, I was making twenty-one pounds something a week, and my dad, who was a time-served engineer, used to be on eighteen pound a week. Mind you, we used to do a lot of overtime. But he was working seven days a week, double time on Sundays and that, and he was having about eighteen pound a week. We were quite well – we had a car from as far back as I can remember. We were the first in the Harlaw Road to have a television, black and white. All the kids would stand outside the gate, and Dad, 'Ah well, let them bring them in', and they would all come up and sit round the telly.

Mill Housing

He [Galloway] built eight houses up what's now the Harlaw Road, the top side of Harlaw Road, and he also built Piano Row. And there was six in Orvale and three opposite the mill. There was two small cottages. I think about twenty-seven [in total]. And then they started buying some of the big houses in the Lanark Road, at the junction of Lanark Road, but that was getting later on.

You just went to the office, and saw the secretary, Mr Mowatt – and then it was Ainslie who took over [as company secretary]. But you just went to him and said, 'Any chance of a mill house?', get your name down and then if one come up you got it. But the ones that my dad was in, they were virtually all people that worked in Portobello, the Fairgreaves, Amises, Haig, Adams, my dad, McMinnagles, Irvine, and there was that Jimmy Aitkinson the beltsman, he come from Portobello. Quite a few had come up from Portobello with the Galloways when they moved out.

We lived in 1 Bavelaw Bank. It was two-bedroom. We were in the top flat. Although it was one up, in the kitchen was a concrete floor, and there was four cupboards, and the two bottom ones were for your coal. I mean it's unhygienic now, because your pantry was above one and the cupboard for the dishes was above the other, but they were above the coal cellar. It was a good house, possibly go for a bomb now.

First Jobs

I went and got in the mill and my first job was on a rewinder. Reels of bond would come off, and they were slit down to sizes, certain sizes, and that was my first job. I done it for quite a few months, and the chap that I worked with, oh, he had a terrible temper. I remember one instance, there was three reels going up – there was one on the top and two on the bottom – and one of them burst, and he threw the spanner and it clipped the two of them into three! I got off my mark and ran to my dad because Jock McMorran, he had an awful temper.

Then I got onto machine cleaner. Everybody wanted on the machines. That was the pinnacle at that time, and I got on as machine cleaner, and that was quite a job. You had to clean the whole frame with a mixture of paraffin and oil. You had to clean the whole frame, and the shake bar where the watery substance comes onto the wire, which was a steel bar along the side. This was done every day. You cleaned the oil off, rubbed it down with emery paper to get rid of any rust, and then oiled it again. Nowadays, it'd be a cardinal sin, the amount of oil that was wasted on that. I remember one time I had done it, and there was a speck o' rust that I had missed. And the assistant manager come and he took his hand and wiped the whole lot off and I had to start again. It was fantastic.

And then I went on as second assistant, getting shells for to run the paper onto, and taking the reels away and putting them in racks, ready for cutting or going to the conditioners. And that's when I had my accident.

My Dad had made these shells about twenty year before.

PAPERMAKING ON THE WATER OF LEITH

They were big shells for a special order that had been made, and you used to wrap the chain round, so that it was locked. But with these shelves, they were so big you could only hook it like a 'U'. And it was getting near the end of the shift, and I was taking it through to the cutter house. Now there was four sets of racks, and you brought it through on the overhead rail, run it into the racks, and then lowered it into place. But when I took this one, the points jammed, it swung up, and the chain come off and hit me on the front of the leg. And if I'd stayed still I suppose I'd have been alright, but of course as far as I was concerned I'd only got a knock, and I went to stand up, and that's what caused the problem.

When they took me to hospital and went to operate, they couldn't get my dungarees off because the bone was sticking out through the back. So they had to cut my dungarees off, and they were going to take my leg off. But because I was only sixteen, Sir John Fraser, who was surgeon to King George V at the time, in Scotland I suppose, he said, 'We'll take a chance', and I had three operations in a fortnight. And it still wasn't right, and I used to go about in a caliper for, oh, about three years. And you go before the board, and they were going to stiffen my leg, make it permanently stiff. And my mum wouldn't have that; she said no.

Once I got reasonably well, I had the caliper on for years. When I went back to see about a job, they gave me a promotion up to the top wire. One of the machines had two wires – the paper come along the bottom, you had paper up the top, they met, went through a roller that was sprayed with starch, and it made a thicker board of that.[1]

I went back on the Sunday night, got everything done – because Sunday night's the messy night – washed all my floor – the floors were washed regular, and the boards along the front that used to reach up. And on the Monday night, everything's all ready, just walking back and forward, checking that the paper running is on the wire, and I slipped on the floor. And now, well, it would've been nothing, but then I was off for another eighteen months. I got thirty-two and six for three years, virtually full pay, and that had to keep me and give me my pocket money.

The Salle and Packing

I went back and they said, look, as things are at the moment I think you should go up to the finishing side. So I went to the salle. I hoped eventually to get back to the machines, because the papermaker is the top man unless you get promotion up to foreman and the likes of that.

John Anderson, he was the papermaker, and Tommy Elliott, he was the assistant. And then there were three foremen – Andrew Fleming was one; I cannae just mind the other two. That was the place you wanted to be, but I was put up to the salle. And I was just helping out in the salle and then eventually I got put onto the packing. And I was packer for quite a wee while.

Tommy Ferguson used to be the head finisher. He was a man and a half, small with glasses. He had an open desk. If one of the girls was standing talking, you wouldn't think he could shout, but anybody at the far end of the salle – and the salle was quite a length – would jump when Tommy Ferguson shouted.

When I started, we used to tie all the packets with tape, and it had to be in a straight line. And if he come and there was one out of line, he would take his knife and cut it. And then you had to lift them off, get this one, pack it in, and the same when we went onto gum tape. I was actually only learning to tie with the tape when gum tape machines, brown gum tape come in, but it was the same thing. Everything had to be in a straight line, and if there was one little line there, he'd get his knife and cut it, so you had to start! But I was on that packing for quite some time.

Tommy Ferguson, he retired. Willie Arthur came from Inveresk and took over the head finisher's job. Willie Arthur says to me, 'How'd you like to go on the guillotine, just to help out', and I said, 'Oh, great.' So I went on the guillotine, and I was on that for a long, long time. Mr Strachan, he became the papermaker, and on the guillotine you were on a bonus. You had your basic wage, and then you could make up to, I think it was eight or nine shillings bonus on the packet. When it went on the guillotine, it went up to eleven and six; you could make an eleven and six bonus.

TIME AND MOTION

And we had the time and motion come in to study us all.[2] It was a London firm brought in to bring this time and motion in. They would stand all day, timing you on every aspect of the job. Lifting the paper, straightening it, putting it in the guillotine, making your chop, turning it, making your chop, turning it again, trimming the four edges and that. And they stood there for hours: taking the pallet away, bring in a new pallet in, putting your wrappers down. If it was bulk-packed, if it was going to be packed in the time it took to straighten it up, and that.

They watched and timed and studied you. I always done a good day's work, and they used to study me more than anybody else. You know, they would study the others, but then the time and motion was always taken off me because I would work away steady. Because I mind Greenhaugh, one of the men: 'Oh,' he says, 'we prefer to study you.'

THALLON VEITCH

They went right through the mill, and out come the new list of points – you got so many points per ream that you were lifting – and they cut it drastically. Cut it away back – we were virtually going to go nearly twice as fast to get the same money. So I went to the head finisher and complained, and Willie Arthur came back and said 'Nope, we can't do anything about it.' So I said, 'Well, I'd like an appointment with Mr Strachan.' So I had the appointment with Mr Strachan – nothing doing. I says I want an appointment with Mr Galloway. Now, that was unheard of, and I says, 'No, I want an appointment with Mr Galloway.'

We got an appointment with him. And he had a massive big leather old-fashioned top desk. I was sitting on one side, and he had all the time and study on his side of the desk, and I had the union man with me, supposed to be fighting my case. And, oh, we argy-bargied, argy-bargied, and then Mr Galloway turns round and says, 'You should be lucky, Veitch. You've got a job.' And I says, 'No, Mr Galloway, you should be quite lucky you've got a worker like me.' I says, 'My timesheets, for all the time I been here, prove to you that I give you a good day's work, and if I don't have a job here, I'll soon get a job somewhere else.' Well, he says, 'Veitch, I know nothing about this, you better go and settle it with them that know.'

And that was the time and study. We got up, 'Thank you', and walked out. I got outside the door, and this Strachan was a big man, about six foot two, he grabbed me by the lapels and pulled me up, and he says, 'Thal, bloody fine, you know you can you do it, get on with it.' I was the only person I think who'd ever been in his office. Nobody went to Galloway. He was a very aloof man, very aloof. At the start, he was in the mill every day, and he would walk around the whole place, everywhere. He never spoke, he would maybe give a little nod of acknowledgement, but he never spoke to anybody. So it was unheard of for anybody to go and want an interview with Mr Galloway, but it worked. We got a slight improvement, but it still meant we had quite a bit more to do.

Unions

Jock Cosser was the union official, and I wasnae happy with the way he reacted. I told him in no uncertain terms. I says, 'You were supposed to be on my side, supportin' me, Jock.' I says, 'All you done was backed up things that they said. You didn't support me at all.' Not long after that, we used to get an increase. Was a farthing an hour or a halfpenny an hour. And the machinemen and machine assistants, they used to get maybe three farthings or maybe a penny an hour. And we had a union meeting in the canteen, and the row was about parity of the wages. The discussion went on for quite a while, and I stood up and I says, 'Well look, the discrepancy between my wages and your wages, every increase is getting larger and larger.' I says, 'Should it no be the same increase across the board? Once you've established the differential, should you no have the same increase across the board?' And Francis Eddington, who was union secretary, he's on about how they were like the top men – the beatermen and beater assistants, and machinemen, machine assistants, they were Grade 1. Guillotine operators were Grade 1A. And oh, I was arguing, arguing, so I got up out of my chair and I walked up to him. I took my union card. I said, 'That's what I think of your union, you're no fightin for me.' And I threw the card and I walked out.

Three months later Jock Cosser come back and convinced me it was beneficial to be in the union. But it used to bug me that we would get maybe a halfpenny or a farthing, and they would get three farthings or a penny an hour. And the gap was widening and widening. But of course that's why you wanted to get on the machines. You wanted to be a machineman or machine assistant, you were on the big money then.

But when I went on as assistant head finisher, when I was starting somebody new, I would say, 'Now there's your union official, go and see him.' Because when I had my accident, there was no union in the mill and they were just negotiating to start, but the union took my case up. And as I say, they were gonna take my leg off because it was such a state. And, well, my mother had this lawyer; they were talking about fifty or sixty pound compensation. I got £875, and that was only because the union fought my case. So when I had a new start coming in to the salle I used to say, 'Now there's your union official, once you get in just go and see him and give him your . . .', because in case of injury it was essential you were in the union, because if you hadn't been in the union you would've got nothing, no in these days. Well, even what I got – £875 – it would have been worth, oh, £150–170,000 now.

Promotion

After a while, they moved the guillotine down into the middle, and the supervisors used to come in the back door that was right next to my guillotine. I was always about my guillotine. David Clifford come in, and he was standing talking – he used to speak away – and he says, 'Davie Haig's gonna be off' (that was the supervisor, the assistant head finisher), 'gonna be off for a while.' And he says, 'D'you fancy the job?' And I says, 'Oh, I wouldnae mind', and he says, 'Right then, you've got till the weekend.' This was the middle of the week, you see, and I says, 'Oh, I'll tell you now, Mr Clifford, I'll take it.'

But I says, 'When Davie Haig comes back, what'll happen to me?' 'Well,' he says, 'we've opened that new salle up the stairs. We're gonna need assistants up there.' We had one big salle, and then they opened a new part through because we were quite busy. And they opened this new part, and he said, 'There will be a position for you on the staff, don't worry about that.' Because I didn't want to take on this position and then maybe in a few months find I was back on the shop floor. 'Oh no,' he says. So I says, 'Right.'

And there was a wee office along the far end of the department, and the boys used to go in it, clean up and get everything all ready, put all the orders in order and everything. And I never said anything, I never told anybody. I went along, told my wife 'I've got the chance', and on the Monday morning I walked in with my sports jacket, flannel, collar and tie. Had the key and just walked in, and the faces, the faces of my workmates, you know, it was amazing, all the mutterings and everything going on. I remember one chap said, 'Just let him tell me, just let him try and tell me, I'll tell him.' And I never bothered.

And you had certain orders that if you could get on quicker than others, you could make your bonus quicker. Big sheets for *Vogue* magazine, you really struggled to get them, and everybody used to leave these orders aside. I just went all round the department, looking. All this was lying about, so I just got a list of the numbers, and I went round everyone and I says, 'Right, I want that order next, I want that order next.' And this chap says, 'Oh, but,' he says, 'I've got more.' And I says, 'Leave it, that's not in a hurry, I want them.' And I got all the bad orders out of the road, and things worked out smashing, just smashing.

In the salle we had 128 girls at one time. There were three girl supervisors, plus Jean Haig – she was like the senior supervisor. Now a salle, they're just parasites, you do nothing for production in a salle, you just discard good paper. So you're reducing production. But going back to these days, it was essential, because people wanted a perfect sheet. Nowadays, you'd get away with the small blemishes, small faint lines that we discarded. It had to be a perfect sheet.

Work Hours

Mill work started on a Sunday night, ten o'clock on a Sunday night, and it worked through until twelve o'clock the following Saturday. It closed at twelve, and we would get out by about one o'clock, and hurry home to get away to the football. Six to two, two to ten, and ten to six: that was the three shifts. Because I remember, when the dance was on a Friday night, I'd go to the dance, and the dancing finished at two, maybe even a curry, then walking from Currie after two, getting into my bed, the next thing my mum would say, 'Come on, Thal, it's half five, get up.' And she would have my porridge and toast for me, get ready, and then I'd be hurrying down the road to get started for six when I was on the machines.

Later, it was half seven to quarter past five, and then it became eight to five. And you used to have to stop at nine for three-quarters of an hour for your breakfast, and quarter to one to half past one for your lunch. Most of them that were on days, they had their snap with them. Initially, when I first started, there was no canteen. But then they did bring one in. They used two bays in the stock room, converted that into a canteen, so we did have it at the finish, but not at the start. If you were on, you took your snap, and to heat the water, you used to get one of the steam pipes, put your jug down beside the steam pipe, and then turn the steam on it to boil your water. It was great, you know, it was a way of life for the village.

There was the mill horn, used to go when it started – if the day shift used to start at seven, it would go at five to seven and then seven o'clock. Then it would go for your breakfast break, and then it would go for your lunch break, and it would go for starting up again. This is the steam horn; it could be heard everywhere, in Kinleith, Kinnauld or something like that. I mean, we lived about a mile up the road and you could hear it. You could set your clock with the time the horn went.

They used to all clock in at the timekeeper's office. You had to file through. When you went for your breakfast you clocked off and then clocked back on again, the same at lunchtime, clocked off. But then, in latter years, they put a clock in the salle. Because with everybody on days, the whole of the mill, all going through, hell, you were losing about ten minutes of your break by the time you were away at the back. By the time you went through and clocked off. So they put a clock into the salle, and you had to stamp your time.

The timekeeper, he was in there and he checked all the cards, take 'em out and put the new cards in and that, for a Monday morning. He used to go across on a Sunday night – he lived just across from the mill – and he went on a Sunday night and put all the new cards in for the Monday, and last thing on Saturday, taking them all out.

We were paid weekly. You went down on Thursday, and Tom, the timekeeper, he stood there and paid out the wages in a wee brown envelope, a brown envelope with your name and clock number. When I went onto staff, it was monthly. Bit of a hardship at the start. But fair enough, they said, look, if you've any problem, come and we'll give you an advance to tide you over until you get settled in.

Holidays and Annual Trips

Now the holiday was an annual trip. That was only when it used to be the one day a year annual holiday, because actually when I started work, you got a week's holiday then. The pipe band would come walking up through the village, up Harlaw Road, and then all round the village, and then everybody would join in and you would walk down to the railway station, get on the train, and then we went away to Rothesay or Dunoon. I remember Rothesay; it was a big glass-domed restaurant, and you went there and you had lunch. Then you went out, and then you went back and had your dinner. And then the train brought you back, and you all made your way. Everybody who had somebody working in the mill was entitled to go on this trip. You know, they must've made some arrangements with bookings because it was a trainload, it was a full trainload! Because I remember Walter Rankin, his mum had got him and Bill – there was two brothers – sailor suits. And I cannae mind, we were well on our way, and Watty put his head out the window, and of course the hat blew away.

When I first started working, I had to work Christmas. When I started having kids, I had to take a morning off, to see the kids opening their presents, because we worked Christmas Day until, oh I'd say sometime in the '60s.

They used to shut the first week in July – the Edinburgh trades – and then as things progressed and it was the first fortnight in July. Because the Edinburgh trades used to be the first week in July, and the Glasgow trades was the second week in July. Fife was the same as Edinburgh, but then when it became the trades fortnight, it was

Edinburgh was the first fortnight in July and Glasgow was the second fortnight in July. You got New Year's Day – we always had New Year's Day – but there was no holidays in between; they were non-existent at the time.

Selling off the Felts
The blanket felts, that's the first ones off, the wet felts, we used to buy them. The other felts were no good, the machine felts, the drying felts. You put your name down to get a blanket felt. Everybody wanted blanket felts. The blanket felts, they were changed quite regular. Some of them used to wear faster than others. Them nearer the drying end hadnae the same pressure on them, so they would last a month, six weeks or that. But they were changed regular and that's what was done on a Saturday afternoon. The machine operator and his assistant they would go in and change felts. Everybody used to get their name down for blanket felt, and especially during the war, you know, it was a good source, save your coupons, your clothing coupons. In fact, I got them when we were married, and my wife blanket-stitched them all, and when I moved to this bungalow I'm in now, they were all in a case, and they went to Bosnia.

The wet felts, well, I'll tell you what they used to do with the couch felts. During the war they used to make slippers, and these were the soles. I remember my mother making slippers from the ordinary blanket felt, the heavy blanket felt she cut for – they must've got a pattern somewhere – and then the couch felt used to be the soles of the slippers.

Rags
When I was up in the salle at the start, we used to make this blotting paper, and we used to buy these big bales of rags,

just a mixture, only for this blotting paper. It was Asa Wass who used to supply the rags – he lived in the same building that Sean Connery lived in Fountainbridge. If you're going from here along Fountainbridge, where the brewery is, that used to be a scrap merchant, Asa Wass, and we used to get these bales.

We had all these big huge bales, and we used to have them in a big wooden chest on wheels. We had girls sitting taking the buttons off – because there were no zips or that, then – taking the buttons off, or any other thing, and taking woollens out, because woollens were no use. So the girls had to go through, open these bales up – they were all strapped up – and then sit and go through that. And linen, cotton, anything like that was alright, but woollen was out – you couldn't use wools. There would be about six around this big wooden chest, cutting, throwing, cleaning it for any button or that, just at the back end of the war. Some of the things you used to find – even wee bits of jewellery. Somebody had discarded a blouse or something like that, and there might be something in it, and they used to – oh, aye – they used to find various things. And sometimes money. Yeah, it was amazing that the girls used to be sitting there, that was all they done during the day, cleaning up, making sure nothing should go through.

And then it went down a chute, a spare chute into another tub at the bottom, and it was put into what was called collar gangs. It was two big stone wheels, and they just revolved around this chest, and it ground up the cloth into fine pulp.

OTHER RAW MATERIAL

Esparto grass was what basically we made our paper from, esparto grass brought in from North Africa. Well, during the war it was difficult, so they used to make paper with straw. That was basically what we made most of the paper with, but you always put in some esparto grass, because as long as you could put some in, it was an esparto-based paper.

We used to have two big sheds where the esparto was in. We had a big fire in one early on when I was there. Well, there was an overhead crane, and they think it was a spark from the crane. But esparto – it's very greasy, waxy – course it just went up. And there was esparto pulp and wood pulp, and we had another fire there, in the pulp shed. The first one with esparto grass was serious; with the pulp it wasn't nearly as bad, because of course they're quarter-ton bales of pulp. And then a number of years later – I would think it would be in the early '60s – they stopped using esparto grass. I'm no sure exactly, because we were on pulp for a long time.

When we used to get the esparto in first, it used to come in by boat to Leith. When a ship came in with esparto, the wagons would be lined up the road from the top of the village, right up to the corner that goes up to Harlaw Road. Just a line of them, maybe two or three days of that until the ship was empty. And it was the same with wood pulp – when the wood pulp come in, there'd be a line of traffic right up the road waiting to get off and unload. When we used to send out the paper originally, it went by boat to London. And then we started dispatching it with the railway, from the yard where the high school is now in Balerno. Then road transport come in – we had two lorries originally, and then we got another. We had three lorries that went down the road to pick the big orders for our own lorries for deliveries. The rest went with Pollock. Pollock used to take the bulk of the goods going out.

This overhead crane with a man in it driving it would bring the esparto from the shed to the digesters – big tanks – and it used to be fed into that. Then caustic soda was added, and it was steam boiled until it got rid of all the wax and all that was cleaned up. And it was a terrible smell! When Bell's was built, if it was damp – because the smell couldnae go up 'cause of low clouds and that – it hung over the whole village, and Bell's used to complain. The mill had been there sixty years before, and they still complained about the smell coming from the mill. I remember that time when Mr Duncan – he was the headman in the office, and he used to go through in the mill with a letter from Bell's: 'What the hell do you think of this? Bell's are complaining about the smell!' You worked in the mill and that was the just the smell, so if you accept it and not be bothered, nobody bothered, you just get on with it. But that was all done away with when they brought the pulp in.

And then it was given a good washing and pumped through into the storage tank. It went from the storage tanks into the potchers – now that was big circular tanks with a roller with blades that chopped it up into fine, fine particles. It was brown, the brown pulp, and then it was bleached. The guy put in the bleach and it just cycled till it come up white. It was pumped from there through into other storage tanks, before it was drawn off to the beaters. The beaters beat it up to the right length of fibres, cause you got to have a length on the fibre for the sheet to knit. To make sure it was white, a pure white at that, it would be bleached again.

Colouring the Paper

It went from there to the storage tanks for the machines. They were at the side and were called the chests. If it was gonna be a colour, it would be drawn off the storage chests onto smaller chests that had an agitator, and they would add the colours to it, whatever colour you were going to use. We used to be doing about three colours a week, at the end of the week. Thursday night, Friday, Saturday morning were generally the colours, because things had to be all washed down – your felts had to be washed to get rid of the dye. At the weekend – you know, Saturday afternoon – that's what the machinemen and machine assistant would be doing; it was drawn into these chests and then the colours were added.

Originally I remember the men used to come up with these wee containers with the dye, just pouring it into the chest – it was all done by hand and they knew just what to add. And then the agitator would just mix it up properly, and then it was just drawn onto the machine, and it went along the wire. You had suction boxes at the end of the wire that drew the majority of the water off. It went through a couch felt – a roller with a big felt jacket on it – and a steel one on the bottom, and that pressed and sucked the majority of the water out. Then it would just feed through the machines and through all the cylinders, for it to dry off.

Paper and Board Exports

We had two machines in Galloways; Number 1 was a single-wire. The paper like milk came onto the wire. Number 2 machine had the twin-wire, the same volume of paper coming through, and the two of them would join together so you got a thick card coming off. We were virtually world-famous for our pulp boards, stiff card. It went all over the world. We used to send quite a lot to Australia, because we had an export packing department in the bottom of the salle. Index board as well, a cheaper version of the pulp board that was done in twice as many colours as the rainbow. We had a variety of that.

When I was on as the assistant head and head finisher with Archie, I used to go down to the office in the morning to go through the mail with the head clerk in the office, Mr Duncan. All the orders that were specifically for just stocks, he would give me them, and they'd come up to salle, and we would write out an order for, say, 50 reams of a colour for Australia for export. You'd go and collect them out of stock and then you put them on a two-wheel barrow. You put a board down, then you put hessian down, and then you put a waterproof wrapper, and then you put an ordinary wrapper down. And then you put so many, you know, working out for the same size of bales.

Accidents in the Mill

We had a fatality in the pulp shed. The pulp was all just stacked up there, a quarter ton in a bale, and this chap was trying to get some down, and they fell on top of him, killed him. There were no, like, health and safety rules at that time, you know. The whole shed was just stacked up with bales one on top of the other. We had another fatality – a belts man, Jimmy Aitkinson. He come from Portobello, and any belt trouble, you sent for Jimmy. And he was joining this belt that had snapped with crocodile joins. They used to tie a pole, a bar onto the side, to guide the belt back onto the pulley, and then they would start it up slow, bring it round to get the belt on, take it off, and that was it. Whoever started it up, started it up quick and the pole come round and smashed him in the skull. We had another one on the machines. I was up in the salle at the time of that, and again the belt had come off. This chap went to put it on, and he was trying to ease it on, and the machine went away and pulled him into the belt.

That was three fatalities during my time, and there was lots of wee accidents. One of them happened fairly regular – the calender rolls, a stack of steel rolls or rubber-coated rolls – you got the paper through, and then you fed it back down the stack. Now you had to push it in with your fingers, keep them clear. There was a bit of a guard, but you still could get your fingers in, because the guard was leaving a space like that, just enough space for paper to go through. That was quite frequent, people cut their fingers.

There were some people who had done a little first aid, no anything really, but latterly we employed a nurse. And we had a first-aid room up in the finishing house at the top. And the nurse was there – Kate [Milne] – she was there till the finish. But in my time they had no first aid then, it was just everybody running to help, trying to help, you know.

Mr Walton and the Off-Machine Coating

Mr Galloway's nephew took over when Mr Galloway retired and then died. There was John Haig, and then he went into semi-retirement and he brought this other chap in, Walton, to run it. Walton went ahead with this off-machine we used on machine coating, and we were one of the first in Britain to take this – it was an American patent.[3] There was a trough, the coating mixture went into this trough, and then there was a blade, and as the paper come through the blade just rubbed it onto the paper, and when it went through the calenders it was impregnated, and then the calenders polished it all up and it come through with a shiny coating. But he had seen this other process – off-machine coating, brush coating. Now, brush coating makes a far better job. It's more expensive, but it's far better. And he had seen this Joseph Eck, so he bought this machine, and we spent a fortune building new premises for it on the other side of the river. He spent a fortune getting this all ready, up-to-minute state-of-the-art machines and everything, but we just didn't have the money for to pay the banks back. The banks come and say, look, well, we've given you the money, you're supposed to pay, we want it back, and that was the cause of Galloway going down. It was a shame because it was a great mill, and we had more orders on the book than I had known.

We just couldn't get to grips with it. I mean it was a massive machine, and you had to run jumbo reels on it, which was in five- or six-, seven-ton reels. You'd have three men on the Joseph Eck, and then you had two on the rewinders. Then you had to wind them down again to go to the cutters. Because the cutters couldnae deal with a jumbo reel. So you know, it was all cost, building up the jumbo reel to six, seven ton, and then running down a jumbo reel back into ton reels. It wasnae cost effective.

Now we made about a one-ton reel, and they had to go through a rewinder, and they were all joined together to make a jumbo reel. And then the jumbo reels went on the Joseph Eck and then same again, it was a flying splice when they joined up. The machine was slowing down, and then when it was getting near the end of two of them we hit together, and away they'd go. But they just had so much trouble trying to get it to go.

I suppose it would have been great, but they just had so much trouble with it, and they couldn't produce the paper quick enough off the machines. Trying to speed up the machines, the rubbish it used to make. Oh, unbelievable.

Promotion to Head Finisher

Archie Mason was the head finisher and taught me a lot when I was assistant to him. I got on with Archie. He was getting a bit sick and that, had a bit of heart trouble, and he said he was gonna resign. Walton sent for me and he said, 'Look, I want you to take on the job as head finisher.' 'Oh,' I says, 'I cannae take Archie's job' – because I'd been friends. And he said, 'You're not taking Archie's job, Archie wants off, pressure's too much for him, and with his troubles now.' And I says, 'Has he got a job?' 'Oh yes, we're gonna have a job for him.' 'Oh,' I said, 'in that case it's alright; I'll take it on.' So I took it on. And we increased tonnage with a bigger salle, and improved production. Wee things, the boards, the girls used to turn it to see what was on the other side of the sheet. Well, we used to flick through, and of course when you're flicking you can see the underside. Turn the board round and flick through the other side, made it quicker. Things were going well. We used to do *Vogue* magazine, a lot for *Country Life,* and there was various sizes and weights.

We used to run trials to improve [paper production]. You couldnae send it out in case something wasn't just right. So I had one stacked up separately, over the reference number and description. I wanted a wee break, so I was going away for a long weekend up to Fort William, where my brother had just started up in the pulp mill. And on the Friday night I went to my assistant – who was Ossie Rinning – and I says, 'Ossie, now watch, when *Country Life* goes out, none of that must go.' I went to the stockkeeper, and then I went to the foreman in charge of dispatch, Jimmy Currie, and I says, 'For goodness sake, Jimmy, watch none of that goes out if *Country Life* goes out this week.' I even went to one of the female supervisors who I had nothing to do with.

I come back late on Monday, and the phone's ringing. And I said to Nan, 'If it's the mill, I'm not in.' 'Is Thal there?' 'No, he's not here at the moment.' About an hour later, the phone. I said, 'Tell them I'm not in,' and I said, 'Oh, for goodness sake', and it went again. I says, 'Oh look, I better go across'.

So I go over to the mill – here they had sent some of the stuff out. The loader had . . . had not checked the reference number – because you sent out according to reference number – and put it on. So I got in Bobby Addams and I says, 'Right, get a telex away immediately for that to be cancelled and send off the correct stuff now.' Well, during the week a telex come back from BPC, British Printing Corporation, about this trial. They werenae supposed to see all this, you know, the wrong order had been sent, and Walton sent for me and he went to town. And I never said anything, that it wasn't my fault, that I wasn't there: I covered up for my staff. And he says, 'If you can't do your job, I'll have to see about somebody who can.' And I says, 'Ah, fair enough', thinking that was it.

On the Monday morning, Davy Elliot – who was the assistant papermaker – come up and says, 'Right, Thal, where are we?' And I says, 'What do you mean, Davy?' He says, 'You're down in charge of dispatch.' Walton had demoted me, and I says, 'What d'you mean, Dave?' and he says, 'I been sent up here to run the salle.' I says, 'Since when?' And he says 'Oh, I was sent for and told to start in the salle Monday morning.' He says, 'You're gonna be in charge of dispatch.' I said, 'Ah, right then, fair enough.'

So that was it. That went on for a wee while. I was in dispatch; after about a fortnight, you know, I was all upset inside and that. And we used to have a morning meeting in the manager's office, and Ian Napier was mill manager at the time. And I says, 'Ian, I want a meeting with Walton.' I never ever got my meeting to this day.

But when East Lancashire come in – we used to buy paper from them because we couldn't cope with the rubbish stuff some of them were making on this Joseph Eck – they thought about buying Galloways. John Seddon – who was the assistant managing director – he come up, and we got a message over the tannoy: 'Would all the senior management go to the work manager's office, please.' And Mr Jones said, 'As from this moment, Mr Walton has no further dealings with John Galloway.' On the following Friday, John Seddon sent for me and says, 'Thal, I've got a bit of a problem.' He says, 'I'm needing somebody to run the salle.' And he says, 'You've been recommended by Mr Jones.'

николаs

Everybody had a nickname. The Martins – there was Old Craw: that was the grandfather, a machine operator. There was young Craw. There was about four generations of Martins, all working in the mill. Wee Wheatley, he was a postman. There was Old Growly – he was a bad-tempered wee man, but he was at the bowling. And then his son, and then his sons were all called Wee Growly – you know, it passed down into Growly's grandson. Oh aye, everybody had nicknames, and that's how you were referred to, even when you went to the door. 'Dooky. This is Paul. Is Dooky in?'

Balerno Community Spirit

Balerno was something special until Galloways shut. It was fantastic! Everybody knew everybody else, and everybody knew everybody's business, and if you were going to see somebody, you knocked on the door and walked in. You never stood waiting. You just knocked on the door and walked into the house – 'Aye, alright?' 'Aye, okay.' – and just discussed your business. Oh aye, the village those days was like one big family.

Closing the Firm

Even when the mill closed, you know, we had more orders on the book than we had ever had. We used to run with orders of about 300 ton. If we had 300 ton in the books – because we only used to make about 150, 160 ton a week – we were in clover. And when the mill went bust, we actually had 500 ton on order.

How were we told? Well, we'd had one or two meetings in the boardroom that things weren't going too well. And you know, they were hoping something would turn up. Well, they knew we had problems, but again I don't think they ever expected it, because Galloways was a name known over Britain and the world for the stuff we supplied. But each meeting seemed to be gloomier and gloomier, and things weren't going too well. And then we had this meeting that Mr Seddon of East Lancs had us all in for, and he told us that the mill was gonna have to close.

They just told us that the mill was closing and that was it, and then they just started laying them off. I was at my wit's end, because there was nothing in Balerno. I hadnae even thought about going up to Edinburgh for a job. I was lucky. I was kept on because all my workers had gone. I had to do virtually all the work. I was there nearly a year running down the stocks. I brought Dave in just to finish, to help out just when I was leaving. Dave and Fred, they come in because orders were still coming in for paper and board that was all in the stock.

We used to have the bottom flat was chock-a-block with stock. It was all on an aisle, the different papers or board, and about twelve aisles, and the board and that was all packed. And then up on the top in the dispatch area, there was a lot of customer stock. We held it, they used to order it and we'd draw off, so that was all there for to get rid of. In fact, the man that I finished up being employed by used to go round mills buying up old stock and machinery. And he come there, but like everything else the receiver wanted as much money as he can to pay the creditors, and Bernard couldnae get anything.

Some of the machinery went to India, but a lot of it was just scrapped, you know, it was just a waste. The Joseph Eck. I'm no sure if Dickinsons finished up with the Joseph Eck. It was a good machine if we could've got it going right, and I'm sure you know it would've made money, but it just took too long to get it going.

In the end, it was dead quiet. I had a dispatch clerk, Ena Ovens, and she just sorted out all the orders and that, and then I would just spend my day going about, getting out, but there was no that many orders really. But whatever was wanted, she would order up the wagons; the wagons would come in, just load it on the wagons and that was it. Oh, it was terrible, actually. I mean up the stair, nothing, just the spiders. I received nine hundred pound and that was my superannuation and redundancy for twenty-eight years' work: nine hundred pound.

After the mill closed there was an awful lot never worked again. I mean, the mill was the soul of the community – that's where 90 per cent of the money for the village came.

So when that went, it must have been catastrophic for some of the businesses in the village.

After Galloways

John Seddon who'd come up from East Lancs, it was him that said, 'If things work out, Thal, I'll send you to America to get up-to-date.' He sent for me one day and says, 'I got a job for you.' Now East Lancs was a big concern, they used to deal in international pulp and paper and board and that. So I assumed a job at East Lancs, and I says, 'Oh, very good, Mr Seddon.' 'Grosvenor Chater, have you heard of them?' 'Oh,' I says, 'We used to make Bavelaw bond here for Grosvenor Chater.' 'Ah well,' he says, 'You'll know them, it's a mill in North Wales.' Now we used to go on holidays to Abergelly and round about that area, and he said, 'I'll tell you what, take two or three days holiday, go down there, see what you think of it, you'll get your salary from the mill, and you'll get all your expenses when you go down.' So Nan and I went down for three days, I think it was.

This mill was out of the ark. I mean, Galloways was quite a modern mill. This was virtually handmade paper. With the potchers there and the beaters there, it went up and down like that, whereas in Galloways it went round in a circle. They went up and down, it was pumped through, and to see if the paper was ready the foreman would go up, take a handful of stuff. He'd rub it through his fingers, say, 'No, give it another ten minutes', or 'Quick, get that dropped, it's ready.' And that's how they did things – it was all done by feel. And I went down and I says, 'It's out of the ark, this place.' And I had a good interview and I got my expenses, and we were put up in a big hotel and all of that, and we enjoyed it. I was back about a week and I said to Nan, I says, 'You know, I could run that job from here. I could run the finishing side from here.' She says, 'Well, if you want to, go for it.' It means everybody's got to be up and away, but she says, 'Well, if you want to.'

Working at Grosvenor Chater

The girls used to take every sheet, pull it in and turn it over like that. Every sheet was turned. I was there just two or three weeks and I says, 'Look, we're gonna start a new system.' I says, 'I want you to flick it up, look at the underside, let it go through. You'll be catching the top side, turn it round and do the same again.' And it just sailed through – tonnage went up. Some of the time the girls were waiting, so one of the first things I had to get rid of was six or seven of the married women. And they were all like Galloways – it was all grandfathers, fathers, mothers, grannies, uncles, aunts, nieces.

So I was very unpopular. But when we started increasing production a bit and that, then I brought them back. And then we run into trouble there, because the Scotsman – his grandfather used to own Inverkeithing Mill – he come there and he done the same as Walton done up here. He brought palo refiners from Brazil, he bought a flow box from Sweden – various things. And it was a small, very small, mill; tiny, about a quarter of the size [of Galloways]. But it was a great place to work – it was a family concern, and they looked after you. Like, at Christmas, they would get maybe an extra half-week's wages, on top of what we were entitled to. There was no money in the mill, but what money come in was spread between the workers, you know. And he started buying all this, and just the very same [as here] – the bank wanted money he'd been spending on this, and they went under. Ah, I enjoyed my time in the mill.

Notes

1. Galloway first installed its twin-wire in 1937, and this system evolved to give the paper two topsides.
2. In 1937 John Galloway & Sons was the first mill on the Water of Leith to call in a work-study firm called British Bedaux.
3. The Champion Process.

Richard Blaikie

Directly from school I did one year's on the farms working as a tractorman. And then I decided it wasn't for me, so I went into the papermills and I got a job in what was Woodhall Mill at the time. What happened was that my father – he was on the farms as well, and we'd been up in Mid Kinleith for twenty-one years – I think at the end of the day they didn't really want to carry on the farming side, and they applied for a council house in Currie and they got a house at 11 Stewart Gardens. And my dad actually knew one of the managers in the mill, and he'd been speaking to him and he said, 'Well, if you'd like a job, come down and see me.' So he came down, and my dad got started. I had a brother that worked there as well. He was in the coating plant. He was in Balerno for quite a few years, then came down to Woodhall on the coating side. And he worked on the coating plant and was there just when it closed in 1984.

My dad was there for about a year I think it was, before I decided to follow in his footsteps and go into the mill. He was on the cutters, actually cutting and wrapping paper. He was a cutterman, and a reeler. We used to make reels as well. With a reeler, when we made reels, we used to put a big roll on the back of a reeler and slit it into different sizes on a cardboard centre. He did that, plus he was a cutterman all these years as well. I worked along with him for about a year. And then a vacancy came up on the paper-making machine. I was an obvious choice, being there, you know, rather than applying for somebody else for it. Because I used to give them a hand on the machines anyway. It was the old-type beaters that they had in these days and there're only about fifteen cylinders on it. And that's how I started off in the papermaking industry.

Woodhall Mill at that time only made wrappers, which was very thin paper that went up to Kinleith Mill and they would cut it into sizes. It was very low-production. I think it was maybe something like five tons a week that they made. Two men could actually lift the rolls that came off the dry end of the machine and store them. They just came off the machine and straight onto a cutting machine, and the cutting machine was all set up for the various sizes they wanted to cut.

Kepper Boy

One of the first jobs that I actually had was what you call a kepper boy. When the paper is cut on the cutting machine, it goes through onto belts. But instead of being stacked in the modern systems, at the end of the cutting machine a boy used to sit on a board and catch every sheet of paper that came down. They came down two at once, and he used to take the two sheets down and he used to kepp, as I say, onto this board, a free right-angle board, so's all the edges were nice and straight. And any defective boards that were coming down on the cutting machine you could see them, and you used to flick them out – like overhauling, like the girls used to do later on. So that was my first job. And then it was lifted out of there manually. They used to flick one side over and the other side over, and you'd take as big a handful as you could manage and lift it out onto another table, and that was flipped over and it was tied at the same time. So there was no pallets of stuff as such built up – they was put onto boards and other things straight away and tied up. And then every morning, the John Bryce contractors used to take it away.[1]

After a couple of years, about 1957, Inveresk bought the mill, to build it into a big board mill. They decided to change it into the Woodhall Paper Board Company, so I started working with them. When they demolished the old mill, I assisted them to take out a lot of the old machinery. But while that was being taking out, the new hydropulpers and everything was being built; they actually kept the mill going most of the time and there was very little downtime at the end of the day.

In the early stages when the new mill was being built, surplus steam was carried from Kinleith Mill. The capacity of their boilers was such it had surplus stream, and they could boost up the system. We only had one boiler at the time in our mill, and this pipeline was built all the way from Kinleith. It travelled a mile – was quite a feat at that time. When Kinleith closed, we were cut off at that time. We had two Cochrane boilers put in, and they kept the mill going after that.

Mill Changes

But anyway, in 1957 they decided to change the mill over and build it all, and then at that time I went off to the RAF for a couple of years' national service. When I came back, the mill was actually running, but it was still in its infancy at that time. They'd extended the buildings out the back – there used to be cottages and small offices outside the back of Woodhall, which they demolished. Then built up the new board shed for storing the pulp and things. Well, the pulp actually got stored outside, but the cardboard, wastepaper, newsprint, that sort of thing was all brought inside. Then they changed from the old beaters into hydropulpers, and they had refiners and stock-clearing systems, and then on to the wet end of the machine, the new paper machine, the board machine.

Because we didn't have a cutting machine, most of the reels of paper was sent through to Westfield Paper Mill that particular time and cut through there. And that again was John Bryce used to bring in these big rolls, and there'd maybe be about five ton in a roll, something like that, three tons in a roll.

We went through by taxi at nighttime and we used to work all night cutting. This is when I came immediately back from the RAF, when I wasn't actually put right on the machines straight away. We used to go through with them, through to Westfield, and come back in the morning. It didn't carry on for all that length of time, going through there – maybe a couple years, eighteen months before the cutting machine was built.

Then we started to build up the continuous cutting machine, with paper that came straight off the machine and straight up through into the cutting machine to cut it as it was being made. We just had the one board machine, but it churned out about two hundred and some tons a week. It was a quite a big job, in comparison to this little wrapper machine that we used to have.

STARTING IN THE MILLS

You went on training courses, but it was more or less hands-on type learning in these days. The apprenticeship was from working on the actual machine. You started off as a felt boy, to a dry-end assistant, to a dryerman, to a machineman, then a shift foreman.

PAPERMAKING ON THE WATER OF LEITH

Sometimes, if they were a wee bit older, just came in from doing another job, maybe they'd go on the tying, or we'd put them on the beaters, or something like that. Or a machine assistant, they could come in as a machine assistant. Sometimes the felt boys didn't always just automatically go up – some of them were just quite happy to do what they were doing. Depended on the individual.

A felt boy just watched the felts that travelled back and forward all the time, depending on the position of the rolls. There's a little screw and you just adjust the roll; if you want the felt to come forward, you screw the roll into the direction that it's coming, and that brings it forward. But you got to check it, so it's got to come right forward, and then you check it back again, because it weren't automatic things in these days – you just had to watch them. The only thing that they didn't have to watch was the Fourdrinier machine, the likes of the wet-end machines – they were on automatic guides, had to be because it was quite an expensive piece of equipment, copper wire. The board machines and that, in these days they didn't have anything automatic. We did eventually get automatic things fitted.

But they would watch out for numerous other things. Look out for things that are happening, maybe the machineman's away doing something else, checking his other end or changing a roll. We used to have a horn, you know at the wet end and the dry end – you just toot the horn and the machineman would come up. We had phones as well, but I mean they used to just blow the horn, if there was a break on the machines. Somebody within that machine area would just ring the klaxon thing and everybody would come in from nowhere.

Moving up the Ranks

When I came back I started on the machines. I started on as they normally do as a machine assistant. When a vacancy came up in the dry end, you went in as a dry-end assistant, as a drierman, so you stayed as a drierman until there was a vacancy on the machines. Those days, nobody overstepped anybody; there was nobody brought in to do a job unless it was a job that nobody else could find anybody to do. But they normally started at the bottom and worked up, from a machine assistant to a drierman to a machineman. And if he was any good as a machineman, he would be promoted to the foreman or shift supervisor. But you did your training in the mills – you went on the cutting section for so long; you learned all about the cutting machines. You did the machines, then you went up into the process plant and you learned all about the beaters and how it processed the pulp, and the distance of chemicals and things like that. You did everything before you got actually put on as shift supervisor.

I did a couple years on the machine, as a machineman, and then a vacancy came up on the management side. I went on to be a shift foreman. But during that time, you maybe got about six months or something like that, just going round various departments, learning everything. The existing beaterman that was there, in the processing plant, I would go up with him. Although I was shift foreman, I was only a trainee foreman if you like. Although I had a good knowledge of it anyway, he would learn you all about making up a batch of pulp and how long to let it run.

Work as a Shift Supervisor

Being responsible for everything during the day, you had a shift report book, which was handed over to you from the previous shift supervisor. He would tell you 'everything's okay' or 'we're having problems with this; we're having problems with that', and his whole shift report would be written out for you. First of all, you would check back his shift report, after he was away, and check out and see what's happened during the day, and then you could just go and maybe ask quality control, 'Oh, how's the product, like is everything okay with it?' You used to get delaminating, which was when the board used to split when you folded it, or cracking if it was overdried, things like that. So you'd have to go and see about all these sort of type of things. You had people who would overall decide whether paper would go out or not. If it was cracking, too bad then – 'I can't let that go to a customer; that goes into stock.'

Then you'd go down to the machines and you'd be checking round your machines, have a word with your machinemen and your driermen, see if everything was running okay. Then you just follow up to the beater flat [floor], have a word with them up there about things – 'How's things going?' sort of type of thing – 'What're you using?' For various jobs you had different mixes of pulp, things like that. So they had a furnish sheet; everything was all made out. If it was of a different quality, they'd have a different furnish sheet – a different recipe, just like baking.

And we'd do a Schopper Reigler, which was the length of time that the water took to drain, which was you had to do the check your fibres were of the proper length.[2] When the paper went through the refiners, this was the last step before it went on the papermaking machine. They'd took these tests, and they put it though this Schopper Reigler. There was gauze in it, the water went through the gauze and left the fibre. It was actually weighed at the end of the time, to determine how free the stock was, and if it was not free enough then you'd increase the cutting on the refiners.

Four-Shift System

The mill, it was quite an interesting place to be in, you know. But there was a lot of change. We used to work a three-shift system at that time, where you closed the mill on a Saturday morning, everything got washed up, and you started up on Sunday night again. But then, it must've been in the '70s, they went onto the continental shift system, where they introduced a four-shift system. And from there they just carried on, and we only shut down about once a month – when things got a bit dirty and they decided to wash up things, change felts and that sort of type of thing – and then start up again.

When you were on a four-shift system, you had staggered holidays. You'd have your days off through the week. After that, you'd work all weekend, and got two days off during the week. Then you go onto a different shift – three shifts was running and the other one shift was off, and then when the other one went off, the ones that were on their days off came on, and so it went on and on, all the time.

If somebody didn't come in, you had to give them a certain time. And if they couldn't get anybody from the shift that's just gone off to cover, they gave you an hour to get somebody. And after that, if you didn't manage to get somebody within an hour – you'd phone around somebody at home on a rest day, something like that – then you could walk off and they couldn't do anything about it, so they just had to run a man short. The other ones used to get extra money – I mean if it was the tying, if they were a man short in the tying – they used to do his work, work harder and get his money split, more or less.

PAPERMAKING ON THE WATER OF LEITH

We'd have maybe twenty a shift, something like that. Maybe six in the cutters, that's counting the cutterman and his assistant. There was five on the papermaking machine. There's a dryman, two assistants, then a machineman and an assistant. The beater house had two pulpermen, a beaterman and then three in the shed – and then the shift supervisor. There were also paper testers as well. There was two paper testers on, worked in the lab. The testers all sat down in the lab, and you had a paper tester who done all that.

Quite a few of them come from the town. There was a lot locally, but there weren't enough locally to keep the place going like. But a lot came from Stenhouse and Wester Hailes, with some from Gilmerton, Polmont or West Calder. A lot of them had their own transport, but on a Sunday morning we used to lay on a transport for them, the ones in town anyway, because there was no buses running at that time, in the morning. If there wasn't a bus laid on for them, it was a taxi – some of them used to get taxis in, and the company paid for it.

What we had was an urn to make your tea, but you carried a sandwich with you, and that's all you had. And when you were on the job, you sat at the side of the machine and you had your sandwich on the job. We didn't have an official break. Very often your tea was left and you went and did all the repair work, and then you carried on after that, with the rest of your sandwiches if you got one. Sometimes it was pretty tough, but most of the time it was alright. I think we had a cooker, like a little grill–cooker thing, you could make a bit of toast or something. But it was all done on the job, and it was like that throughout. Although when things ran quite well, I had maybe two or three cups of tea during a shift, 'cause I could fit it in, as long as the work was getting done.

RICHARD BLAIKIE

CHANGING FELTS
A felt used to last about eight weeks, between seven and eight weeks, if it was a good felt, and that was quite a task to change one of them – used to take about four hours or some five, six hours. You'd take all the front of the rolls off the machine framing, slip through these big presses, take fronts off the presses, and then lift them up with tackles and slip the felt underneath. Quite a big job!

MACHINE BREAKDOWNS
If you had any trouble at all, like breaks in the machines, you were there to assist, to give them a hand to get things going again. We had cylinders that used to go out of line continually, causing the paper to break. You'd find there was a cylinder out of line, it had sprung its ratchets, sprockets, and the machine had to be shut down for that. We'd also have a cylinder shearing and falling down in the pit – very dangerous.

You used to have your little accidents with the felts as well, bursting halfway through a shift and closing everything down. Then it was all hands on deck, even the cutting assistants and the cutterman tiers, five tiers on a shift, something like that. They would come down and give you a hand, change the felt. There were spells, sometimes, when things didn't run too long. You maybe filled up the pit underneath the machine with broke, which is just waste paper that fills up, due to breaks on the machine through some kind of fault – maybe bad edges on deckle straps sticking out catching on the machine and splitting the guiding rope. Or the coating on the edges of some of the cylinders used to build up, gradually splitting the edges of the board, so when it dried out it used to burst, break.

PAPERMAKING ON THE WATER OF LEITH

Sometimes you couldn't wash up 'cause all the systems were full, you know, emergency shutdowns. When the electric board went on strike, we could only manufacture paper for three days a week, and close down again. And we used to get a lot of trip-outs as well – the system used to trip out and everything on the machines used to stop. And that was a mess. Pulp used to run everywhere 'cause it was gravity-fed, and it'd just boil over everything. Till you get sorted out, valves closed. Even boiler problems would close us down. We used to have boiler problems as well, maybe the bricks coming away from inside the boilers, things like that. And they would have to get all done.

THE SHEDS
There used to be three people in the sheds. They used to have overhead cranes at one time, back in the early '70s. It was overhead cranes in the shed, and they handled everything by hooking the bales onto the crane with wires. And then they introduced reach trucks after that – one of these diesel forktrucks, it had clamps on the front – and they used to just drive into the bales, put the clamps in, lift them up and then put them onto an elevator that went up to the hydropulpers. Often the people who worked in the shed were quite old, like, you know, getting on a bit, so when they introduced trucks it was quite technical for them, but they took to it very well, like a duck to water, really. 'Cause you had one man up in the crane originally, and the other one would be climbing over the bales and hooking them on, which was antiquated, and then they introduced these reach trucks, so they could just put the prongs up, put them straight in and clamp them, lift them, and then put them on.

RICHARD BLAIKIE

WOODHALL BOARD PRODUCTION

The main board [produced] had three layers to the board: you had the waste paper in the back, which was a cardboard and newsprint mix; and you had mechanical wood pulp, which was an unbleached pulp, or you had bleached pulp; you had the sulphites, which was hard woods cut for craft pulp. And with these three you blended them in, so you had three layers in the actual board when it came off. Like a shoe, if you take a shoebox, an existing shoebox just now, you'll have a white liner on it, which is the good one for printing, and then underneath that you'll see that it's pale yellow, and then you got your cardboard backing.

Then we introduced a coating plant as well, that came in the early '70s. Everything seemed to happen in the '70s, round about then anyway. And the coating plant was built. Three operatives – one man on each shift in the coating plant. And that was quite a thing for a board machine at one time, because they had to alter all the run of the board, make it double back on itself through the coating plant to catch it. So we had two of them, and it was quite successful, because it was cheaper to use china clay as opposed to wood pulp, which was very expensive. But the clay filled in and gave a better printing surface.

BLINKBONNY POND

Up in Blinkbonny we had a pond, and that used to fill up with water, and because it was higher than the mill we needed a flow of water down from it. The funny thing was we had a lake that came off the Water of Leith, into where the boilerhouse was, and that water was pumped up to this pond, which was a high pond and gave us the gravity to feed everything in the mill. At the back end of the year, when all the leaves used to fall, the leaves used to come down and choke everything up. We used to run out of water 'cause there was no water getting pumped up to the pond, and the pond used to empty. So you had somebody up there all the time trying to clean all the leaves away, keep all the water in it, pump it up. It was usually the boilerman's job to keep his eye on it, which was quite a feat, watching his boilers and scraping leaves out of this thing.

Practical Jokes

There was quite a good atmosphere in the mill; it was quite a good laugh. You maybe heard this one before about people getting married. There used to be a great thing to get hold of the person that was getting married shortly and give them a great goin' over with dye and things like that. That's what they used to do with them: used to strip them and put dye on them. Another thing we used to do occasionally: somebody would doze off somewhere on a machine or in a little corner somewhere – you would find them on the night shift, especially – you used to get all rub dye on your hand, like that, 'cause being in the mill was quite hot – you used to blow the dye onto their faces, and them sweating, they used to wake up all blue, you know.

Social Activities

We had a social club, and I ran the social club at that particular time. And we had a fishing club which somebody else ran, and I was the secretary as well, and we used to have a monthly outing to Loch Leven or Loch Fitty. To go there we used to sell football tickets for about five pence or ten pence per ticket. And to promote that you had to get permission from Fettes police station – they had to give you permission to do this sort of type of gambling. So I had tickets with my name on it: R. Blaikie, Promoter. You picked out two numbers I think it was, or you wrote down two numbers, I cannae remember how it actually worked now. It was to do with the football sweeps, Sunday morning results, and so on. Maybe about thirty chances to win something on it. And we used to sell them on the shift, and that's how we got our money to pay for our trips to Loch Leven, because it was quite expensive.

We had a football team as well: that was another thing they did have, a football team. Somebody else used to run that; I think John Anderson, he had to do with football. John was quite a good football player. Tom Daly, there was quite a few of them – the football team used to play other mills. The social club also ran a golf club. Tom Daly used to run the golf club, and they had their outings. Also we had an annual dance – at that particular time we were quite in the habit of going to the Glenburn, which was up past Blinkbonny, and they used to run their dances up there. We used to have to pick a menu, if you like, go up and pick a menu for Christmas dinner, things like that, and have the dance. And there was usually quite a good turnout. All the managers used to come; everyone mucked in and had a good night. It was subsidised – the firm gave us so much money towards it, but we also we paid so much. We paid maybe, I don't know, six pound or something a head, a couple, something like that.

Works Visits

During training we used to go up to Aberdeen, up to Mossy Mill and these places, because they were board machines. If you were interested, you could go on organised trips the mill used to do. To a certain extent you could go round, but you wouldn't really get into intricate details or anything like that. You wouldnae get to see the furnish sheets, how they produced the pulp for the board. We weren't allowed to see that; neither would they when they came to our mill. We used to get trips from other paper and board mills. They would come to our place and they wouldn't be allowed to see furnishes, but they could walk round and see the equipment and things, cleaning systems, see what kinds of refiners and hydropulpers that we've got, and systems for loading up, the pulpers and the length of times that we pulped it. But that would be about it.

We didn't really encourage school parties – it was not a very safe place, working in a papermill, for kids. A lot of things can happen very quick in papermills, because you've not really got a lot of room. I mean, you've got a paper-making machine and normally you're only about two metres from the machine to the wall – that's all you've got to work on. So if there's any problems on the machine with the broke, or anything has to be thrown out, you've only got a small area to work safely. You're tripping over things half the time – it's not the safest of places to work.

Health and Safety
I think it was 1974, something like that, that the Health and Safety Act came out. There was an act out before that, away back, whereby a factory inspector would come out and examine things. I mean, normally when there was an accident they would come out and they would say, 'Well, you'll have to do something for this area here; that is a danger.' But after legislation came out, we had to tighten up on safety. Everything that looked dangerous had to be cordonned off, or safety guards put in front of it. Like in press sections, when the presses were first put in there was just an open press – you had two large rollers and a felt went through there, with no guards on the front. They were

unguarded at one time – we've had people put their hand through, accidental, most of them young lads who were doing felts and things like that. So they were all tightened up and guarded. Everything had to be guarded. Sometimes guards on the papermaking machine were so well guarded that they were a hazard in themselves, because you couldn't operate things properly because of guards, and it made it just about as dangerous.

We didn't wear headphones. The beater flat – that was one of the ongoing things – it was I think at the latter end they were provided with earmuffs, but a lot of them couldn't wear them anyway. After they came up above too many decibels we were supposed to wear them, and I think that a lot of people who actually worked in these conditions, in later years they turned quite deaf.

Accidents

I was on the machines at the time when one of the young lads put his arm through a press. He lost a lot of his fingers. There was two or three of them who got caught on what you call a drum reel. At the end, all finished paper's wound onto a big roll, and that's all shell where the paper's wound onto. It's a steel-case thing, with spindles on either end, and that sits on a drum, and it turns the same speed as the machine does. But you've got to hand-feed paper onto this shell, and often quite a few of them put their hand right in. Of course, they burnt their hands from the friction. They were taken away and had to get skin grafts on all their hands, because the friction burned the backs of their hands. The young lads, there was quite a lot of them, quite a few of them having been nipped in there.

But the calenders were another matter. I mean, I got my hands cut on the calenders as well, and had to go to hospital for mine. We had a jam stack at the calenders – where there was a break on the machine and a lot of debris had come through the calenders, and the last lot that come through was soft and still wet, and jammed the calenders. You get the bottom roll still turning, which is the driving roll, the ones above it stop. You can actually create a flat if it runs so long on a bit like that. So the calenders were all lifted, 'cause they're automatically lifted, but this paper was too thick and I had a scraper and I was chippin' away, just taking this stuff out of the rolls, and the roller's still going. Suddenly, swoosh! Hand went straight in. It was caught, but it wouldn't go through the rollers, 'cause there was a finger guard on. But I broke that finger, nearly pulled it off, had many stitches in there, peeled that nail right off and burst it all, and I had to go to hospital. I was off for about a fortnight, three weeks something like that.

Working Conditions

It was very hot; all departments were very hot. When the paper actually came off the machine, it went up about 20 feet through a hole in the wall. The cutting machine would pick it up and it'd be brought in across. The papermaking machine gave off heat from the cylinders floating in the air and the cutting machine, because it was higher than the actual papermaking machine. The heat was something wicked. And even in the beater flat as well, that was higher than the actual paper machine in these places, and the heat used to rise and spread all over the place, you know.

At the latter end we had fans put in. Your paper had to be a certain condition for packaging, and we used to bring it from a hot atmosphere when it was packaged, shrunk-wrap. We used to get a polythene sheet, pull it out to a certain length which would fit over a pallet maybe 6 feet high, pull it down and put that into a shrink-packaging machine. It was then taken from there down into a cold atmosphere downstairs, and that used to create a lot of condensation within the wrappers.

It wasn't the best of conditions, because the way that Woodhall was, they didn't have the storage space. After the paper was made, it was brought downstairs to ground level, where the sections were open. It was quite cold in that part, and the paper used to stay there all night, and it was taken away in the morning. By the time it got to a customer, sometimes it would get a bit of condensation, especially if the board was a bit high in moisture to start off with. You can run with intolerances, but the higher the moisture was, the more it'd have to give off.

Returns and Rejects
There was always stuff getting returned, but I wouldn't say there was a tremendously high percentage of it, but there was a lot returned at times. It depends if it was a great big order – you could maybe get an order of fifty tons, if a customer wasn't happy with it. You used to get an uneven moisture in a board, which would cause it to go wavy, and moisture content was another important factor when it went through a printing machine on a first run. I didn't know all that much about the printing, but I learnt that you ran a sheet through a printing machine at certain temperatures. Everything's all sort of controlled – atmospheric pressure, temperature and things – and if you run one through and the moisture was too high in the board, then it would give off moisture that would shrink the board. So when it passed through the second colour, one colour would overlap the other and they couldn't use it. So that would get back to the mill.

PAPERMAKING ON THE WATER OF LEITH

They wouldn't have printed it all – they'd have printed so many piles, maybe tried to persevere with it – but we would sort it all through. Some of it would maybe go to somewhere else, go to another customer. It depended what they were going to be using it for, you see. Sometimes if it was only for a one print, it might be okay. But there again, when we're making boards like that, when it's an unstable moisture on it, even when it went through the converters for packaging you would get cracking on it, and you would also get a soft board, or it would shrink. Moisture was a very critical thing. Even if there were debris in amongst the sheets on the pallets that went out, a bit of paper or cardboard overlooked, and it went through their printing machine and jammed up their press, it'd cost a lot of money. Plus their blankets and things like that.

What happened after that then, of course at the latter end, they computerised the whole machine. Woodhall was bought over by GP Inveresk, who computerised the whole system, which was a very clever idea. It really took over, probably be about the turn of 1980. They actually paid for the computing system, which is about a million pound, I think, to do that. It made a big difference. It was quite a complicated thing at that particular time, because nobody was sort of geared up with computing systems. Introducing computers helped a lot, but there were still times when maybe a bad felt – a dirty felt, if you want – wasnae properly cleaned, and that particular strip maybe wouldnae drain – the computer couldnae pick that up. You could take the moisture head and move it to any part of the board machine cross the way. And you'd maybe just keep it there on that particular part, and the computer would actually work to that specific area that it was picking up moisture on. It could be a bit further over which wasn't so good with moisture. So that was just some of the problems that we had.

Our set-up: the paper was actually cut through a fluid jet system on the cutters. A disk would normally cut slitters. This was a water jet – I think it did 2,000 lbs per square inch, something like that. We found that that would keep the dust down, and it kept the dust down to a certain extent, but I feel sometimes that just that very edge sort of made a wee bit damp, made a bad shape sometimes. If you've got a problem with them, the cuttermen were continually having to change jets, and things like that. But the machine, believe it or not, when it closed down, I would say through experience, that it was running better than it ever did in its life. By the end, it'd run and run and run. We had eliminated lots of problems on the machine. They were still making money, but because it was a small mill, it was chickenfeed.

I think that's why it was closed – it wasn't worth all the hassle for the profits that they made at the end of the day, to continue producing it. Plus, the pressures from abroad, with boards coming in from abroad – from Scandinavia and countries – that were far superior, far more stable board. I think it's quite sad in a way, really, when the mill closed, like, because it was running very well, and there were plenty of orders as well. We still had plenty of orders, but we'd never had short time for the lack of orders even up until we closed.

Trouble at Mill
It'd been rumoured for quite a while that things weren't too well. Because of the size of the mill, it's not a big turnover for an American firm.[3] I mean, they like to make millions and millions of pounds profit, not just under a

million, or a million, something like that. It's chickenfeed to them, plus all the repairs. I don't think they were losing money at the end – they were still making money, but not enough to make it viable. We couldn't expand; there was no room to expand anything. If they had had the ground, they could've expanded somewhere. I mean, they did quite well in the area. If you see the area there now, it's hard to believe that actual board machines were there, beater house, a finishing house and a storage place all on that area. But it was too small – I think that's why a lot of paper mills went. These little paper mills now that are still running because nobody makes that type of paper – unlined chipboard just for a basic wrapper – it's not an expensive paper, but there's a demand for it. It keeps them going, and anybody that has got big machines are not making it because it wouldn't be viable for them to make it, but a lot of these little mills have run on. The one at Mid Calder there was run on basically the same sort of thing as I was doing in the 1950s. That's the same type of paper they make, but there's a demand for that, a small demand that keeps these people employed and they make a bit of money. But at the latter end, I think, because it was too small, it wasn't making enough money and just ground to a halt at the end.

I think that towards the latter end, pressures were on everybody because there were an abundancy of mills, and they weren't very profitable. You had mills from abroad, and cheaper papers coming in the country. Wood pulps were very expensive to come into this country – they were making it on hand, and you know things weren't too good. There was a lot of pressure on everybody at the latter end. I would say from about 1980 to 1984, when it closed down, it was quite a lot of pressure.

RICHARD BLAIKIE

We had lots of meetings and things like that with the senior management. Everybody, all the supervisors, if you like, production managers, were all under a great deal of pressure. We had a general manager at the time who was under great pressure, and he would put a lot of pressure on you to get the best results out of you, in a threatening way. It was quite horrendous at times. You were brought into an office and you didn't even know if you were going to have a job when you went home in the morning. That was the kind of sort of pressure you were put under, because a lot of orders had been returned, due to some fault, maybe – cracking or shrinkage. I'm frightened to say it: there was plenty of times I went to work and, as a lot of the other ones, you didn't know whether you were gonnae have a job at the end of the day, plus we knew that it was going to close, eventually within so many months, probably a year to so many months.

Now being in the mills as long as that, you were entitled to a redundancy payment. We didn't know we were going to get a redundancy payment, because you didn't know if you were going to be there, at the end. A lot of the staff, although they lost a good job, were quite relieved at the end of the day – if they were still there, they got a bit of redundancy. They were all paid off at the end, because the mill shut. But they didn't get rid of anybody; in fact it was very difficult at the end. The people that were there – there was not a big turnover of labour – people that were there had been there for quite a few years, and there was very few vacancies at the end.

It closed in the January of 1984, and we were told just before the New Year. I remember quite clearly, it was only about a fortnight, just before we went on our holiday. That was the shutdown, and then they started up and run out the systems after the holidays, after the New Year holidays, and then closed the machines. Everything shut down and washed up and that was it.

The likes of Bryces, some of the local shops, things like that, must've felt a big difference [when the mill closed]. Arthur Scott, who had the Kinleith Arms, must've felt a big difference, because everybody used to go there after work, and most of us went there. Plus the bakers, Allison's the bakers at the top of the road, [we] always used to go up there and get all our bakeries. It's not there now; there's a little fish shop there now. But that closed as well. But there'd be a lot of local places would find a big difference, because the money wouldn't be getting spent. It makes you wonder where all these people go to, whether all of them get work. I think at that time, I mean I would be forty-eight at the time, something like that, forty-six or something like that, when the mill closed, and work was very, very difficult to get in these days at that time. Now everybody's a lot of them my age, older too. But I managed to get a job with Scottish Gas, was very fortunate, but I was with them for ten years after that.

Notes

1. John Bryce: a transport and haulage company, subcontractor to Woodhall.
2. A test to check the freeness of the pulp.
3. GP Inveresk took over Woodhall in 1981.

William Nelson

I LEFT George Heriot's [school] in 1939 and went into Edinburgh Corporation transport department, and was the manager's office boy to begin with until I was called up in 1941. When I came back, the burgh chamberlain, who was in charge of personnel matters over all Edinburgh, had a scheme whereby one could get what is in effect day release to attend either a college or university. I went to Edinburgh University. And I got my fees paid, first of all because I was a foundationer at Heriot's, which meant, you know, I had lost my father early on. So I was a foundationer getting free schooling and free books and a grant to buy my uniform every year.

I finished off my degree, and of course although the burgh chamberlain encouraged his staff to go and get educated, all he could give them at the end of the day was a £10 per annum increase in salary. There were no great jobs straight away – one had to live a long time and gradually get up the chain of command. So most of us who had taken the opportunity to get some kind of qualification moved out of the corporation transport department. Especially after the war, of course, when everything was very much more active – new places opening up. So I just applied for some jobs and applied for this job in Galloways which was described as 'book-keeper'.

The company secretary, Mr Robert A. Mowatt, was a delightful old gentleman. I reckoned at that time when he interviewed me he'd be in his late sixties. I can't remember much about the interview, to be honest, except that the appointment letter said, 'punctuality I appreciate'.

Well, my responsibilities were twofold. One was what you might call keeping the ordinary books – not the private ledger, which was upstairs with Mr Mowatt. I kept the general ledger and the sales ledger, and I supervised the girls who did other kind of book-keeping jobs in the office. And I decided what to pay away in the way of our liabilities to various suppliers at the end of the month. I received the cash from the bank on a Thursday morning and checked it to make sure it was correct, filled the pay envelopes with the help of two girls, and distributed the pay packets at the appointed time at the end of shifts, or at the end of the day from the pay office down below. Most of the papermills tend to pay on a Thursday; I don't know why. That left the wives able to do a shop on the Friday, I suppose.

I found my job quite interesting, apart from, of course, applying my theoretical accountancy to my ledgers and helping the company secretary to finish off the final accounts at the end of the year. I found being involved with the sales side and the production side very interesting, and I'm glad I did it there, because when I went to Caldwells, the two functions were quite separate. And I surprised some of the people in the sales-cum-production side by knowing some of the technical words used by the papermakers, which I was very glad about.

Office Workers

There was Mr Mowatt, Mr Duncan, Mr Nelson [himself]. There was a timekeeper – he didn't work in the office, but he was part of the administration of time and wages. We had a time clock, of course. They started time clocks, and their cards went up to three girls in what we call the wages office now. I didn't have much to do with supervision of the girls in the wages office. Mr Duncan had been in the paper trade for donkey's years, knew all about rules and regulations, about how many people got paid, or how much they got paid. So he kept his eye on the girls, and the girls, if they had a problem, went to see Mr Duncan.

Apart from the three girls in the wages office, we'd five girls in my office, the general office. I was in one corner of the office, so there were five girls and me in the corner. Some of them took part in the writing up of the customers' orders, the completion of the customers' orders, and played a part in the book-keeping side, keeping a ledger or invoicing. Then there was a door into Mr Duncan's office. He had his own office.

And we had sloping top desks and high stools. We had a brass rail in front of you, too, welded on hooks – or raised on hooks, it would be, since it was brass with supporting pillars – and the sloping top desk lifted up. On these two brass hooks, you all had round rulers – these are rods of black ebony. And they are the most difficult thing to use. Then the other thing we had was a papermaker's rule. Now, a papermaker's rule is a specialised slide rule. You know the principles of slide rules, where you have wee things that slide in and out. Well, these were made of kind of bamboo. They were about that width [3 to 4 inches wide, 30 inches long], and they had a top and bottom rail, and they had this bit that slid out and in. Because you had to convert whatever your customer wanted in the size of this piece of paper. You'd have to convert that to the standard size that they ran machines to. And the standard size at

Balerno was 17 by 22 [inches]. So you used this slide rule to convert. In my machine order book I had to write up the order as it came in, and show the conversion to standard size, and take it down to the machine room again.

Mr Duncan would bounce out of his office and want a girl to do something, and of course – seniority – he got what he wanted, but otherwise the girls had all their routines to do. When I entered an order in the machine order book, then there was another girl entered them in the finishing house book, because the finishing house had to comply with the customers' orders as to how the papers were packed, number of sheets in a ream, etc. And the finishing house was responsible for – after packing the paper – getting it on a lorry and getting it out the door, properly addressed.

SATELLITE OFFICES

We had a London office that was responsible for most of our orders.[1] We had an agent in Belgium, and we had an agent in Manchester. Manchester and Liverpool taken together, there's a lot of work done there and a lot of paper needed.

In London, the chief salesman – and he eventually became a director – was one by the name of Freddy MacDonald, who was a son-in-law of John Galloway. And, of course, as a salesman he was a kind of flamboyant character, which all salesmen need to be. Now, I am sure he must have had a secretary–typist, we just called them. And given a secretary, I'm sure they must have had an office girl as well, but I can't remember.

There was a daily letter came in from the Manchester agent, a daily letter came up from the London sales office, and Mr Duncan sorted them out. They were all a lot of queries about possible orders, or about actual orders which had been placed and which weren't yet supplied, and why weren't they being supplied. So Mr Duncan had to jot down on the paper the information about the order, and it went into John Galloway, who sat and looked at it and probably spoke about some of them to the chief papermaker or to the finishing house or whatever – to keep them on their toes. So it was a busy office, Mr Duncan's.

Paying Wages
I was involved in the paying out of the cash at the Thursday. It came from the bank about ten o'clock in the morning. And we'd a stack of envelopes and a stack of money, and the wages girls prepared the envelopes. Took us maybe an hour and a half or so to fill them. I used to go down at two o'clock to pay the shift that was coming off and the shift that was coming in. Then I went down again at I suppose quarter to five or five o'clock to pay the day men – that would be the engineers. I had to make a trip to Mrs Paton in the finishing house office with this box to pay the finishing house girls. The finishing house office had a window to pay them out. It was a box with compartments in it, and it was quite heavy when it was full.

Cost Sheets and Paper Orders
I started off in June 1948, and I'm not very clear as the extent to which Paper Control was still being applied, but it hadn't long stopped.[2] There was a chief clerk who was senior to me, and he looked after the day-to-day correspondence with London and Manchester, Dublin sales offices. And he did the cost sheets at the end of the week and the end of the month. And he kept his eye on me to make sure I didn't do anything wrong.

PAPERMAKING ON THE WATER OF LEITH

The company secretary, Mr Mowatt, was responsible for supervising my work. Book-keeping was only half my job – the other half of the job was operating to the chief clerk and entering up customers' orders in a sales order book, then transferring them to a machine order book, which today would be called a production order for the workers down below.

They were entered in the machine order book in sections, and the craft of papermaking is to run similar kinds of paper consecutively. The machines have different deckles – widths – so that for economic reasons you move from an order with, say, 40-inch deckle to an order with 38-inch deckle to an order with 36-inch deckle, depending on the size of the paper that had been ordered. The other thing you've to make sure is that the colour of the paper flows naturally from one shade to another shade. So you don't make a deep blue and then a deep pink. We didn't do many tints – mainly white – but white comes in a lot of different shades; there's blue whites and red whites and creamy whites. And then there's surfaces – matt surfaces and glossy surfaces.

So the skill of the papermakers is to economically run one order after another to suit their style. It doesn't always tie up with which sales customer has been promised the order in the first place. There was a continual battle between the papermaker, who wanted to remain economical in his running the paper machines, and Mr Duncan, the chief clerk, who stood on behalf of all the sales customers up and down the UK who had been promised their order on a certain day or week. And he wanted to know why they werenae making the paper today.

I got involved in that when Mr Duncan was on his holiday, and I can recall going down to the papermaker in the machine room and saying, 'Such-and-such a customer wants to know when he's getting that order number so-and-so', and I was grabbed by the lapels and almost thrown down the machine room by the papermaker to say he would make that bloody order when he wanted to make that bloody order. But at one time the demand for paper – not so much immediately after the war, but in the years I was there – was such that there was an involuntary rationing scheme. Not run by the government, but run by all the different papermills trying to keep each of the sales customers happy.

It was the time at which the customer – now all customers want their paper tomorrow, you know – but they have to be put on the order book, and then the papermaker has to decide when he's going to make it having regard to the promises he's told about. He doesn't always pay any attention to them. If the paper doesn't arrive when the customer thinks it's going to arrive, then of course he gets on the blower. And Mr Duncan was the man who took all the phone calls and had to keep the customers happy, and at the same time lean a wee bit heavily on the papermaker, who was a very important man – he was a director of Galloways – a man by the name of John Anderson when I first went there. He was a very polite gentleman; he was anxious to make the paper economical, and to keep the customers happy. Most people in the industry are something like that.

Mill Working Hours
Generally speaking, on the three-shift system the basic hours were forty-two on average. But it means that one shift had about two or three hours extra, and another shift had about two or three hours short, so that shifts finished at

a sensible time. The kind of tradition was that they stopped making paper about any time between six o'clock and eight o'clock in the morning, and then they washed up the machines every Saturday.

So the mill ran continuously to Saturday, and then they did that. Now, sometimes on the Saturday they needed to renew things like felts and wires, which are fundamental, and that involved engineers and the papermakers removing and putting on new felts or new wires. So Saturday morning was a busy morning. And then the mill would nominally close about twelve o'clock. But that is a kind of general pattern; I wouldn't like to swear what happened. I didn't go down the mill at that time on a Saturday morning; I might have got showered with water.

Papermaking Machines
We were a fine-paper mill, which meant we made writing papers. We had two papermaking machines. One was a twin-wire machine, which makes slightly stiffer paper called card that has two right sides, because the two wrong sides are stuck together in the process.[3] So you come out with a very nice card for display purposes, and these were all sold to high-class stationers or printers for printing high-class books. The other machine was one of the earliest machine-coated paper producers. These were used for labels and glossy magazines. Coating a paper is putting a layer of china clay on top of the paper. That used to be a separate operation; after the paper was made and dried, you coated it with a layer of china clay. But round about the end of the war we got hold of a patent from America, which meant that before the paper was finished being made a coating of china clay was applied, and then the whole thing was dried off, and that meant it was very much more economical.

Now, it didn't give quite as good a finish as the real art paper, as we called it, but it did give a very good, economical finish. And I would think that most of the glossy papers you see today in publications and things are machine-coated papers.[4]

The papermaking process is interesting – the paper going across over all the wheels [cylinders], and it moves pretty fast. If there's a break in the paper, the men have to attend to this, organise the paper coming off at great speed and lead the tail through. If there was a serious break, I would keep clear of the machine room; you don't want to stand and look at it [even] if he [the papermaker] seems in a good mood. If you go down and find a machine covered in broke, and it's been tearing or they cannae get the tail through and they're knee-deep, shoulder-deep, then you sometimes say, 'You're making a lot of good paper today, then, are you?' But you have to dash out quickly!

Esparto Boiling and Recovery Rates

Coming back to economics, there was a row of esparto boilers. I don't know how many esparto boilers were at Galloways; it might have only been two. But the esparto was boiled, so you had a team of workers on the esparto plant. And there was a chemist closely supervised that, because the economics of doing it was to make sure your recovery rate was a certain figure. Now the recovery rate related to the recovery of part of the soda – the caustic soda to be used again.

So you always had to apply new caustic soda, but depending on the efficiency of the plant you could recover some of that caustic soda and use that again. I wouldn't like to quote a figure of the recovery rate that they were all looking at. The chemist had to take samples of the rate nearly all day long. And a report went in to the managing director of the recovery rate daily. I sometimes saw the figures, but I wasn't much involved in it. Speaking from memory, it was something in between 60 per cent or 68 per cent – there would be two or three percentages' difference from time to time.

And of course, out of the steam boilers that powered the mill you got high-pressure steam and low-pressure steam. The high-pressure steam ran a turbine, to provide electricity, and the low-pressure steam went to heat the drying cylinders on the paper machine and the esparto grass plant. Now, I'm hoping I'm remembering my chemistry.

Esparto Wax

Wax does come out of esparto. I'm not quite sure how, but they managed to collect it and we sent it to Tullis Russell in Fife, because they had agreed to become a centre for what you might call refining the wax – they had a wax-refining machine.[5] Esparto mills were peculiar to Scotland; I don't think there were many esparto mills in England. But it was one of the distinguishing characteristics of many mills in Scotland: they had esparto and made esparto papers. So this wax, what we found – ours was probably pretty gritty with bits of the esparto grass and dust and things in it – we sent it to Tullis Russell from time to time, and they had a plant which refined it. Once a year we got a statement back from Tullis Russell with our share of the surplus, because they sold it to somebody. I don't know who they sold it to.

Leftover Felts

There was a demand [for used cotton and woollen felts], especially after the war when you couldn't get heavy, strong textiles. I have a story that the directors often ended up with nice felt overcoats, and I certainly got a couple of felts. We had a house in Polwarth Crescent – I got the felts, and of course they tended to need washed. If you said you wanted a felt, and they decided that it's your turn to get a felt, they kinda washed it specially. We made curtains for a big bay window we had: top-flight [top-floor] house in Polwarth Crescent, Edinburgh.

Mill Jobs and Experience

I got on well with the foreman, Thomas Elliot. He'd been in the paper trade all his life. And they tended to get into the mill because their fathers and big brothers worked in the mill, and shifted about from mill to mill from time to time, but otherwise they were in a mill for their life. You've to remember that most papermills are up-country. And that means that they tended to be in villages. You can imagine before the war Balerno was, oh, far away from Edinburgh. There was a bus service that ran out to Balerno certainly; the SMT buses went out by Colinton. But I would think that people in Balerno saw themselves as being in Balerno, and not part of Edinburgh as they are now. And that meant that families got their daughters and sons in. The girls would go into the finishing house. Except any girl who showed a wee bit more schooling would end up in the office. And the boys would go into the mill, would be wanting to be a machineman, but they'd have to start off as a machine assistant we called them, the young ones. And when somebody else died or moved out they would get the job if they had enough experience to be a machineman.

Or they could go into the beaters. There were a few people in the beater house. And they could become a beater assistant, and they could be a beaterman. And a beaterman and a machineman were the two key men in the mill because of their experience. The grass boilermen weren't as important as the finished piece of paper. As long as they boiled the grass, that was all they had to do. But the craft of the machineman was to know when to add a little more heat to the cylinders, or to keep it running a little faster or a little slower to make a good finished paper in accordance with the customer sample. Now, you don't learn that overnight, you know; you have to be in the job a long time. And the beaterman, his skill depended on the length of time he allowed the fibres to be beaten – what I think they called 'dropping the beater'. In other words, saying, 'That's beaten enough', open a valve and it goes down into a chest – a storage chest for when it needs to be used.

THE CHEMISTS

We had what we called the chief chemist. He'd been through the papermaking schools and what is now called Napier University. That was the one that was in Chambers Street in my day. They'd all done the equivalent of ONCs and HNCs.[6] That was the chief chemist. He had, I think, two boys, lab assistants we called them. If you were a lab assistant, you had to go to night school. They would be heading for HNC or ONC or City and Guilds, or whatever it was called in those days. They took samples of coal, samples of wood pulp, samples of grass, and tested it to make sure it was in accordance with what was ordered. And they took samples of paper and carried out tests on them. So they were kept pretty busy running backwards and forwards. When I was there they built a new lab in accordance with more modern practices, more modern testing machinery.

WILLIAM NELSON

Job Skills
Papermaking was still a craft skill. I think that the best of them [the mill employees], their fathers or big brothers had been in the mill and knew about the papermaking, what it was all about, and that was passed down. I wouldn't be surprised if the foreman from time to time divulged some information – he had picked up his trade just from what he had worked at. He'd probably been a machineman before he became a foreman. The foreman and the Chief papermaker between them wrote up the daily orders, what machine orders we were going to make next. Each of them would have their particular knowledge.

Transport
We had what was a big lorry in these days; I think it was a fifteen-tonner. They'd had smaller lorries before that, but I think prior to the war – well, even just before I left – trains came up for goods only to Balerno station. And that meant we had wee lorries that shifted the wood pulp and esparto grass and anything else from the train into the mill. But then they closed the railway even for freight traffic.[7] So that meant we bought a fifteen-tonner, and we used two other smaller lorries sometimes for taking paper down to London Scottish Lines in Leith docks. This fifteen-tonner mainly just went up and down between Leith docks and the mill.

A lot of the traffic to London went on London Scottish Lines. I think they had two boats: one left at five o'clock every night approximately, sailed down to London, unloaded, and another one left London at that time and came up. Now that was just general traffic – not only paper – but we always had goods on the London Scottish Lines boat to London. Then, of course, we used other road hauliers – there was a Smith and Saunders. They carried our paper on road to the UK.

There was another function of one of the lorries. Papermaking results in a lot of sludge – that's fine fibres that fall through the straining devices; don't get into the paper. They hold a lot of water, and we had a sludge pond, a settling pond for the sludge to settle down. When it's reasonably dry, surplus water is pumped away, and this sludge is semi-solid and has to be shovelled out of the pit onto the smaller lorries and taken up. I think there was a tip someplace up in the hills. And it's dumped and it gradually dries off. So we had two small lorries and the big lorry. They were kept fully employed and they all had their own drivers, of course. They were mainly day-shift lorries. I don't think they worked overnight, or anything like that.

John Galloway

I had spells when Mr Duncan was on holiday of doing it [reporting to Mr Galloway], you know. You always felt that no matter how much information you put down on a piece of paper, before it went in to John Galloway he always thought of something else he needed to know. He would buzz out about this order for Spicer's, so I had to go and find out the information either from the finishing house or from the papermakers.[8] That was the day-to-day kind of meeting I had with John Galloway.

He was elderly, of course, to my way of thinking. He had been the son of the chief at St Andrews, Guardbridge Paper Mill. And he thought he was likely to succeed at Guardbridge after somebody passed on or retired. Now, this is second-hand information, but the story goes that he didn't succeed, and so he decided to make his own mill. The first place he started out papermaking was an old mill where the Portobello outdoor bathing pool was built eventually.

And the story goes that he left there because of the system in the old mill. There used to be a holding tank above the Figgate Burn. Now, the Figgate Burn runs down into the sea at Portobello. And one of the duties of the night watchman was to open a plug in the bottom of this tank, a big concrete tank, and let the waste product out into the Figgate Burn when it went down and spread itself across the beach at Portobello. I'm talking about before the war, when the controls were not very good, but Edinburgh Corporation had taken power to control the pollution and effluent in all the waters under the area. So it put pressure on Galloway's mill at Portobello, and made his life so difficult that he decided it was no use making paper out there anymore – he couldn't dispose of the waste at an economical price.

So he moved out to the papermill at Balerno, which had at one time been making newspaper for the *Scotsman*. And he ran into the same Edinburgh Corporation who had powers to control the pollution in the Water of Leith. And there used to be a man come out from Edinburgh Corporation daily, and he visited our mill and went to measure effluent that they would allow to go into the sewer in the Water of Leith. He'd make a report if we exceeded a certain amount. And so that became very troublesome too. And this wee man went right down the Water of Leith, I understand, checking up on everybody.

There had been a promise of a new sewer to go from Balerno down to the new housing schemes at Currie, Juniper Green and Sighthill, picking up the waste and sludge and what have you and get it into some kind of disposal plant someplace – I don't know where. We're talking about after the war when I was there. But there was a stringent time for government or local authority expenditure, and John Galloway had to write to Sir Stafford Cripps and his MP about why we had to build in this sewer. You know, it had been planned for a long time, but there wasn't much money in government coffers and so on. Sir Stafford Cripps was a very mean man and he wasnae going to build this sewer. It was eventually built.

Occasionally he'd [Mr Galloway] walk down the mill to see how the machines were rolling, and if he was down there he probably had at the back of his mind asking the papermaker about some special order that we'd been fortunate to collect. How was it doing? When were they starting it? When were they going to finish it? He'd have the chief engineer sometimes in to to ask him was that electric motor starting yet, or was it not in yet? Things like that. He was a shyish man. He wasn't a typical leader of industry in the modern sense. So he'd go down and he'd find Mr Anderson the papermaker, and talk to him. I don't think he'd be above talking to Tam Elliot the foreman, if he found Tam Elliot first. He didn't come into the general office to have a look at us at all, or anything like that.

He didn't have a son. He had this son-in-law, Freddy MacDonald, in London. And then we had this nephew. Now, the tie-in between this nephew, John Haig, was that Jack Haig came from Dairsie, which is in Fife, not too far from Guardbridge, so maybe he was a branch of the family who had experience of the paper trade at Guardbridge.[9]

Holidays

I got paid holidays as a staff member. I would think it would be a fortnight. And in those days the mills didn't close on Christmas Day; they ran through Christmas Day. But there was a habit creeping in, even in remote papermills, of half the staff coming in on Christmas Day and half the staff coming in on New Year's Day.

The mill would get a holiday on New Year's Day, but it was a necessity for some people to be in the office. We had a London office, which wasn't stopping on a New Year's Day. So that's why we needed some people in on New Year's Day. Now, I had been brought up an Episcopalian – so we held Christmas dear – so I always took the Christmas Day off, and I would go in on New Year's Day if required. There would be some essential people doing something on the works side, and not many staff would be in – just a few clerks and clerkesses to answer the phone.

THE GALLOWAY LAYOUT

There was the main building, which was the machine room, basically. It stretched back from the road. Before you went into the machine room, there was the office building, which is beautiful red sandstone, lovely building, mahogany panels in the corridors and staircase. And then you went through the back door downstairs into the machine room. So I don't think it was the same building, but they were closely allied and they stretched back. And beyond that there was the esparto grass boiler house and the main steam boiler house, which of course was an industrial building. The finishing house would be a separate building, in my memory. And it was at the back end – you had to go through all these other places to get to the finishing house. Now the whole history of building a papermill – remember they started off 250 years ago, say in the middle of the eighteenth century – so that they built them to a certain size to begin with, and as the mills expanded they added buildings here and buildings there, and they laid more pipes here and more pipes there. They all became just a heap of buildings, kind of all joined on together; but with various ways of getting from one building to another and upstairs and through a hole in the wall.

They had a long history of office people not supposed to wander through the buildings. I had done the Highers in chemistry, physics and natural sciences, so I was fairly interested in all sorts of things, and I found the papermaking process very interesting. I limited myself first of all just to going down into the machine room because I was looking for the machine order book so that I could fill it up, or going out and asking a question about a particular order. I got on quite well with most of the people. And I think in the first few days I was there, they had a chief engineer to take me round the mill. You know, in the first few days in a big rambling building, you go through and you don't remember where you've been. You know – that's a steam boiler; I'd never seen a steam boiler before. But I found it very interesting.

Getting to Work

I travelled on the bus. I had to walk for the Balerno bus. Now to get on to that bus I had to walk down Polwarth Crescent, Yeaman Place, Dundee Street way and along Angle Park Terrace to the bus when it came up Ardmillan Terrace and shot along the Slateford Road. These were SMT buses when I first started. However, with my interest in cycling, I thought that all my pals commuted to work on their bicycles – not many of them were book-keepers, though.

So I decided to cycle out to Balerno from Polwarth Crescent – that was five miles. Importantly, too, it was up a hill. Balerno Bank Paper Mill was at 500 feet. But I must say it made me a reasonably good cyclist, and of course you are always pushing in the morning to get there in time because of Mr Mowatt's wonderful phrase ['punctuality much appreciated']. And I travelled in a three-piece lounge suit and collar and tie.

NAMES OF PAPERS

[The paper sizes had] silly names. Double elephant, double demy – that was 17 by 22. A lot of the names seem to have a kind of French connection because of the Fourdrinier machine started off in France. But nowadays you talk about A4 – these are modern designations – but before that in offices we all used either quarto, which was 8 by 10 inches, or foolscap, which was 8 by 13.

The whole paper trade was like that; they had all sorts of queer names. And then there was a quarto of this, and double this. And it even went more strange because in some mills – and some particular areas of the United Kingdom – when you quoted a size there was an extra half inch each way in it. So you had to be very careful when you took up a customer's order of what he's actually wanting. So the acknowledgements went out, I think I'm right in saying, to a customer. After you'd entered it up, it went up to the girl to type an acknowledgement. The acknowledgement went out to a customer in size – you know, real size: inches.

What I call 8 by 10 inches, most stationers call quarto in the days for typewriting papers. When I was at Saddler's transport in Leith, I had a filing system like most people, and I liked to see a filing system neat and tidy. So I wanted sheets of paper which were 8 by 10 inches. So I ordered up on the stationer 8 by 10 inches, and it came in and it wasnae 8 by 10 inches, it was 8.5 by 11. And I refused the order.

'Oh,' he says, 'That's quarto – everybody knows that that's quarto.' I says, 'Everybody doesn't know it's quarto – I ordered 8 by 10 inches and I want 8 by 10 inches.' It was 'medium quarto'.

Now, that confusion ran through all the paper trade. Away back, the paper trade in theory went to decimalisation, long before anybody else thought of it. And HMSO converted all its orders into grams per square metre: gsm. And they quoted their sizes in centimetres, and grams per square metre for the weight of the paper. And all their orders came in like that. So all the orders from HMSO, ever since I can remember when I went in in '48, all came in centimetres and gsms. That was a wonderful thing, standardisation.

But the paper trade, the actual producers, didn't convert. I don't know if they've converted yet. They're still talking about double demy, or large post and things like that, and double elephant. Quad demy, you see, becomes a sheet about 30 by 40, which is a big sheet about the size of this table.

Mistaken Order

When Mr Duncan was on holiday, I converted an order form for playing cards – they were to be made for eventual use in South America. It was a very prestigious order and quite a remunerative order. However, the order came in centimetres, and of course we were still running on inches in Scotland. So I'd to convert that. Normally, when Sandy Duncan was doing it, he'd convert it and he'd give it to me to check. And I'd give it back to him. But of course Sandy Duncan not being there, I just converted, entered it up in the book and it went down, and it was made to slightly the wrong size. So there was an awful big waste in that order. And I remember this news broke when Sandy Duncan was away, and of course John Galloway must have rung the bell for me, and I've gone through and had to explain to him what had happened and I'd made a mistake.

Well, he told me off in mild sort of way, 'Oh, you shouldn't have done that. You should have had it checked, you could have it checked by the assistant managing director' – which was a nephew of his, one by the name of John Haig. So he didn't dock my pay or anything like that, but I was very careful in the future. That was the only time I ever got into trouble.

Mill Housing

Sandy Duncan had started off at Polton Mill. And then he had travelled by motorbike daily to Kilbagie Mill, Kincardine. And then he got this job in Balerno, long before my time. He was well into papermaking in all its various guises, and he'd always gone into the clerical side, obviously. He had a mill house up just on the Lanark Road. And the mill had divided a big villa, and John Jones the chemist, he lived in the other half of that villa. Mr Mowatt had his own house close by there. John Galloway lived in Corstorphine, and Haig came from Edinburgh someplace too. And I came out from Edinburgh. Eventually we got a clerkess who came out from Edinburgh too.

A lot of the foremen were in mill houses. It had been a long tradition – because mills are up-country – if you want some people to staff your mills. And, of course, you can imagine that as the mills expanded and started, there weren't enough people in villages to run them until they had property to put newcomers in. I can't recall the actual number of mill houses we had at Balerno, but I can think of most of the foremen were in mill houses. Now, that was the papermaking foreman; there would be an engineer foreman; there would be the chief electrician, who was a working electrician in my day. The timekeeper had a house at the door of the mill, not in the block but just across. There was a driveway at the motor entrance, and at the other side of the driveway was two semi-detached villas. In one there was the gateman – I can't remember his name now – and in the other was the foreman electrician.

They were right on site. If you were a foreman electrician, you turned up at any time of the night or day. Because the other thing is that they had electricians standing by when they started up a mill on the Monday morning. You've got a whole lot of engineers standing by for this and that, because they have to load up the turbine gradually. So they've got the technical experts standing by as well as the papermakers. Well, there was the chief chemist and Sandy Duncan.

I got married in '54, aye, so I lived with my mother until she died in '52. I stayed on in the house and eventually decided to sell it, and my brother and I shared the proceeds when I got married. So I moved out to Hailes Terrace – that's Kingsknowe, half-way up the Lanark Road. And I bought the house and I told Mr Mowatt my change of address. 'Mr Nelson, I'm very disappointed in you. Why didn't you ask me for a mill house?'

Now, mill houses are very advantageous economically, but they have some distinct disadvantages because, if you come in at a certain level, you'll get a certain size of house. And if you get promotion to another level, you're supposed to shift out of the smaller house into a bigger house. And I thought that was a terrible thing, so I wasn't keen on getting a mill house. If I'd got a mill house, I would be living in Balerno. Now there's nothing wrong with living in Balerno, but at the same time you don't want to be under the thumb of your boss.

And the other thing was, that meant if you wanted some decoration done you had to go to the company secretary, Mr Mowatt, and say, 'Mr Mowatt, can I have a painter, could you organise the painting for me', because we had mill painters. They had to paint the mill, and paint the machinery where necessary, and they also had to keep the mill houses in decoration. And, of course, the mill electrical engineers too, they looked after any electric problem in the house, if they could be spared, as it were. And we had plumbers, because there is water flowing every place in a papermill. And we had joiners, because an awful lot of the equipment in those days was made of wood and the joiners just knocked it up. And a lot of the rollers in the machines are made of wood as well, so they had to be repaired from time to time. So, if you get a mill house – provided you can cope with having to go to somebody and ask for repairs – you can get repairs and modifications done alright.

And of course the other problem is that wives want things done, they want things changed. And of course it means that they persuade their husband to go and see somebody about it. And that can cause rifts between husband and wife too. Because some men don't like going and pestering a boss with a thing.

Mill Excursion and Social Occasions

The one thing that the mill provided was an excursion every year – paid by the mill. And it was a train excursion originally in the old days, when there was still passenger trains from Balerno. I didn't go on any of the mill outings – they were wild affairs. And it was up to the workers. They were allowed to choose where to go, and one of their favourite choices was South Shields. Apparently, that was as far as they could get and back in the time allotted. And the purpose of this mill trip was to get as drunk as you could on the train both going and coming. And of course they took their families. I suppose some of the families went down to the beach, but the boys seem to spend their time drinking. They had a restaurant car put on, and usually they had to get the restaurant car restocked to come back. So the stories go. I never went.

There was an annual dance in the later years of my time there. I can't remember an annual dance in the earlier years when I was still in the winching [courting] situation, because I don't remember ever taking a girlfriend to a Galloway's Balerno dance. I remember Fred Ainslie and his wife and Jean and I being at an annual – I can't tell you where it was. It wouldn't have been Balerno; it would be someplace in Edinburgh, and I think that would be substantially paid by the management as well.

Unions and Strikes

During the war, John Galloway had joined the Employers Federation, which was concerned with wages in conjunction with the trade union. John Galloway joined mainly for the purpose of trade union organisation and agreements. I don't know what percentage of workers were members of the union. But I think it was fairly popular and fairly common. There were sometimes threats of strikes, but I can't recall a strike. And that was because, well, in the two mills I was in, the relationship between the bosses and the workers was fairly good. And the workers were very conscious of the needs of the customer. Not so much in Galloways, Balerno, but certainly in Inverkeithing. We had a salesman there who had a great passion for bringing up customers to walk round the mill and see the process.[10] In the hope that he'd land a bigger order, you know. So, when a customer came round the mill, they'd be taken down to the machine room. They'd be introduced to the machineman. And sometimes a customer was able to look at his own paper being made. And some of our machine foremen we had, about six machine foremen at Caldwells, they were on speaking terms with some of our regular customers.

Now, when you get that sort of arrangement, the workers don't feel like having a strike just for fun. The other thing is, the management knew that if there was a strike, they are losing an awful lot of money when you've got a big paper machine standing idle instead of making paper. So there was negotiation and they got something. And the negotiation wasn't done so much at local mills but at group level, the federation and the union talking to each other.

HEALTH AND SAFETY

We had the Health and Safety Executive by; they were called the factory inspectors, came out to inspect the place and see the chief engineer, the works manager, and draw attention to problems. Even in those days we were supposed to have guards on places, but it's very difficult to organise guards on heavy production machinery. And, just as in recent years, sometimes either the workers or the foremen leave a guard off, or tell somebody to carry on working even if the guards not in position. Now that happens, and if they're caught, they're fined.

I remember we had one of the finishing house lads, Fred, he was a first-aid man; he worked shifting bales of paper around. Fred, he delighted in his first aid and putting arms and legs back together again. I remember Sandy Duncan telling me Fred had to attend an accident where one of the machinemen had his hand caught in the nip, between one roller and another. And the hand was drawn in until it pulled out of its socket. Now there was a guard – it was a bar of metal that was supposed to forbid your fingers to go into that nip. But you know, these things happened in papermills from time to time. I think that arm drawn out of the socket story was before my time. But accidents can happen with fast-moving and heavy machinery. You just don't stop a roller rolling if it's going along.

Leaving the Galloway Mill
Now, you see, when I went in there I found myself with Mr Mowatt, as we called him, and Mr Duncan and myself. Mr Duncan had vast experience of the paper trade. He did the cost thing, and he had been in my job before his predecessor had died and Mr Duncan had stepped up. I was a BComm at that time, Edinburgh University, and I had done the same accountancy course in Edinburgh University as the CAs were doing in those days. So I felt that when Mr Mowatt retired I would have a good chance of succeeding him as the company secretary. Because by that time Mr Duncan would be a bit older too. That was my thought. And of course in these days, when we were into a job, you thought you were going to be there for ever more.

However, what happened was that a firm that had been the auditor of Galloways, Balerno, one of the partners in it became a director of Balerno, and this chartered accountant on the board of directors looked round for a successor to Mr Mowatt, and it was Fred Ainslie – one of their employees. He was a good accountant – he'd been in the auditing profession, and so he was looking to get out into industry. So Fred Ainslie's name was put forward as an assistant secretary to take over from Mr Mowatt when he retired. I realised that my avenues were closed. And while Mr Duncan's job would have been quite a good job, it didnae seem to be the kind of job that I had a BComm for. So I came across this advertisement for assistant secretary at Caldwells. I applied for the job and I was lucky to get it, and so I moved.

NOTES
1. In 1933, Galloway opened a London office at 2 Creed Lane.
2. Paper Control was a government body that took over the industry during the war years and determined what could be produced.
3. In 1937 Galloway installed a twin-wire machine. This system gave a paper two topsides through two webs working simultaneously and joined together in the suction press to become one sheet of paper.
4. The Champion Process.
5. Tullis Russell Paper Mill, Guardbridge, Fife.
6. Ordinary National Certificates and Higher National Certificates.
7. The Balerno Line closed for freight traffic in 1967.
8. Paper merchants.
9. John Haig was assistant managing director of John Galloway.
10. The Caldwell Paper Mill, Inverkeithing.

Glossary

Agitator	A revolving paddle used in *stuff* chests or vats to mix and keep the pulp stirred.
Beater	A device invented in mid-seventeenth century Holland that superseded the older method of preparing the pulp by hammering and stamping rags in a mortar.
Broke	Paper that for some reason never made it to the end of the papermaking process. It was usually taken back and fed back into the *potcher* at the beginning of the papermaking process.
Caliper	The thickness of a sheet of paper or board, measured by a micrometer and usually expressed in thousandths of a millimetre.
Calender	A set or stack of rollers or rolls between which the paper passes and is smoothed by their weight. The calender is placed at the end of the paper machine, while the supercalender is separate. Both may have heated rollers.
Casein	Obtained from curdled milk and used as an adhesive in the manufacture of coated paper.
Caustic Soda	This is added to *esparto grass* while it is in the boilers to break down the fibres into cellulose.
Champion Process	Process involving a twin-*wire* machine that produced paper with two top sides.

GLOSSARY

Cutterhouse	Area in the mill where the cutting machines are located.
Digester	A vessel where woodchips, *esparto grass* or rags are boiled and mixed with chemicals.
Deckle	In hand papermaking, this is the removable frame around the mould that helps to retain the pulp on the mould's surface while the water drains through. On a *Fourdrinier* machine, the deckle straps perform the same function on the moving *wire*.
Esparto grass	A tough grass grown in North Africa and Spain used as a raw material in papermaking.
Finishing house	A department in the mill dedicated to overhauling the finished paper before dispatch.
Felts	As used in papermaking, these are a woven material of either cotton or wool with a raised surface that supports the wet sheet of paper during the stages of removal of water and, on a machine, during the subsequent drying.
Fourdrinier	The standard papermaking machine, providing a single continuous process, named after the brothers who financed its early development.
Galart	A paper made by the John Galloway mill. It was a coated paper made by continuous process on a twin-*wire* machine.
Galitho	An art paper made at the John Galloway mill.
HMSO	Her Majesty's Stationery Office.
Loading	Mineral matter (china clay, titanium oxide, etc.) introduced into papers and boards at the *beater* stage to give improved finish, printing quality and colour.
Overhauling	The stage in the process when paper is checked for flaws and inconsistencies.
Palo Refiner	A machine that chops fibres to the required length for use in the papermaking process.

Potcher	One of a series of *beaters* or engines used in washing and preparing raw materials, especially *esparto grass*, for processing into a pulp.
Presspâté	A machine similar to the wet end of the *Fourdrinier* machine that was used to turn wood pulp into sheets.
Pug	An electric shunter engine.
Ream	A quantity of sheets of paper, usually around 480.
Reel	The revolving frame or drum that receives the paper coming off the machine.
Shade	Paper that is not the exact colour needed for an order.
Salle	A department in the papermill dedicated to *overhauling* the finished paper before dispatch.
Slake	To dissolve lime by combining it chemically with water.
Stuff	Paper stock or pulp ready for making into paper.
Turbine house	The area in the mill where the turbines are located.
Wire	A shortened form of 'machine wire', referring to that part of the *Fourdrinier* machine on which the sheet of paper is actually formed.